Billy the Kid's Courthouse

The Construction, History, and Preservation of an American Architectural Treasure

By Tim Roberts and Billy Roberts

The Historic Lincoln County Courthouse as it looked c.1874

Maps by Billy Roberts, Illustrated by Igor Olszewski

Edited by Gregory Scott Smith, Ashley Roberts, and J.M. Roberts

CONTENTS

This book is dedicated to the men and women who labored tirelessly and selflessly to preserve the Historic Lincoln County Courthouse and to those who continue to protect Lincoln from the progress of time. Thank you to all of the researchers who have inspired us by dedicating their lives to increasing our understanding of Lincoln's role in the complex tale of the American West, including Frederick Nolan, Robert Utley, Nora Henn, Drew Gomber, Maurice Fulton, and many others.

A special thank you to the following individuals and organizations for their assistance in making this book possible: Ms. Gwendolyn Rogers and the Lincoln County Historical Society; the Staff of the University of New Mexico, Center for Southwest Research; the Staff of the University of Arizona Special Collections Library; the Staff of the Lincoln Historic Site Archives; the Staff of the Fray Angélico Chávez History Library.

FOREWORD

Upon entering the stairwell of the historic Courthouse in Lincoln, New Mexico, your gaze is drawn to a small hole blasted into the western wall. For millions of visitors over the past eight decades, this unassuming scar marks the end of their journey to walk in the footsteps of an American legend. While this purported bullet hole lies at the end of many peoples' odyssey, for the authors of this book, it represented the beginning—the start of a journey to try and tell a complete story of the Historic Lincoln County Courthouse and give the structure the recognition it deserves. Like the Courthouse, the bullet hole is a physical connection to the past, specifically to Thursday, April 28th, 1881. On that day, William H. Bonney, better known as Billy the Kid, escaped his meeting with the hangman, killing two deputies and possibly leaving a grizzly calling card on the western wall of the Courthouse. On that day more than 140 years ago, a violent jailbreak catapulted a young outlaw into the national spotlight and secured the Historic Lincoln Courthouse's lofty place among the pantheon of American heritage sites.

The origin of the legendary bullet hole, or possibly holes, is a complicated tale and the ideal place to start this story. For at least four decades after the Courthouse opened as a museum, two bullet holes adorned the wall with interpretative signs describing them as

The only authenticated image of Billy the Kid, taken c.1879/80 in Fort Sumner, New Mexico
Photographer unknown
Public Domain

authentic. Many believe the scars on the wall are genuinely the murderous handiwork of Billy the Kid, while others doubt their authenticity entirely. It is undeniable that the bullet holes existed for at least some time after that fateful day in April 1881—as the existence of at least one is verified by the very man under whose watch Billy the Kid escaped, Sheriff Patrick F. Garrett. Although highly exaggerated, Garrett's commercially successful 1882 book, The Authentic Life of Billy the Kid, does provide us with the famed lawman's account of the Courthouse crime scene in the days following the violent incident. Garrett mentions explicitly that at least one of Billy's bullets had "...passed through his (Bell's) body and buried itself in an adobe on his left."[1] Two years after Garrett's investigation of the Courthouse, the new Sheriff of Lincoln County, John William Poe, moved into the upstairs living quarters along with his new wife, Sophie. In her memoirs Buckboard Days, Sophie Poe describes the Courthouse in great detail, including the recollection that there were still blood stains in the stairwell—a grizzly reminder of Billy the Kid's murderous escape. Interestingly, she does not mention any bullet scars, but it seems unlikely that county officials would have repaired the holes while leaving blood stains along the walls and floors. Garrett and Poe's accounts of the bullet holes and blood stains represent the earliest and last known references to the scars until well into the Twentieth Century.

In 2016, staff at the Lincoln Historic Site published an article in *El Palacio* magazine, seemingly putting the question finally to rest. In the article, the author shared an excerpt from a recently received letter from the daughter of former curators John and Caroline Davis. The letter provided the following account of how the holes came to exist.

> *As to the bullet hole—I know it's a subject of a lot of rumors and stories, but I have the answer! There was fresh plaster on that wall. Peter Hurd convinced my father (John Davis) that the smooth surface was unauthentic. So my dad shot at the wall and made it authentic…the stories are always more interesting than the fact.*[2]

With help from her husband, John, Caroline Davis served as the Courthouse Museum's curator between the fall of 1950 and the summer of 1952. According to their daughter's memory, this would place the genesis of the famed bullet holes sometime between those dates. This accounting appeared to settle the matter once and for all, and since 2016,

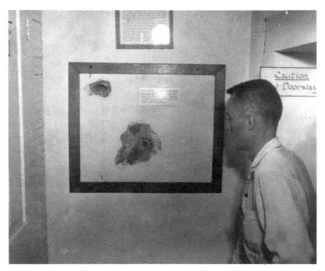

Curator John Davis admiring his predecessor John Sinclair's interpretive description of the purported bullet holes, c.1951
Lincoln County Historical Society

staff and volunteers have shared this information with understandingly disappointed guests. However, this explanation has always proved problematic, as references to the bullet scars predate Davis' tenure in Lincoln. In fact, within the pages of Walter Noble Burns' The Saga of Billy the Kid, one of the earliest modern mentions of the feature is made. Copyrighted in 1925 and released in 1926, Burns primarily based his retelling of Billy's story on questionable first-hand accounts backed up by even more unreliable "research" conducted by Burns and others. While the factual nature of the book is less than desirable, its impact on the expansion of Billy the Kid's legendary status is undeniable. In chapter two of his book, Burns described the current state of the town of Lincoln, presumably in the early-1920s. In his description of the Courthouse, Burns stated, "At the foot of the stairway inside the dingy old building, you will find the hole in the wall made by the Kid's bullet after it had passed through Deputy Bell's heart."[3] Inspired by this dubious account, we set out to track down as much information as possible regarding the famed bullet holes and to establish their origins once and for all—ultimately leading to previously undiscovered evidence that breathed life back into the legend of Billy the Kid's violent escape.

Working backward from the 1950s, we started with documents left behind by the Courthouse Museum's first permanent curator, John Sinclair. His original drafts for interpretive panels for the museum were among his correspondence and notes. One of the elements Sinclair chose to highlight was none other than Billy the Kid's bullet holes. There was now no doubt that Julie Davis' memory was not one-hundred percent accurate. Perhaps as a six or seven-year child, she remembered her father and Peter Hurd re-interpreting the bullet holes or even placing a new glass frame over them that covered them for many years. Regardless, the scars undoubtedly existed before the 1950s. Sinclair's interpretive panel that adorned the wall informed visitors that,

These are the actual bullet holes made by Billy the Kid on April 28th, 1881, while imprisoned in the room above and sentenced to be executed on May 13th, 1881, for the murder of Sheriff Brady, when he shot and killed one of his jailers, James Bell. This incident took place as the Kid made his famous escape from this building; the shots were fired from the stairs, Bell fell dead at the foot. The hole on the upper left was made by the final shot.[4]

Further substantiating Sinclair's work, the August 4, 1941 issue of *LIFE Magazine* provides photographic evidence of the bullet holes and his interpretive panel. The article "Truth About Billy the Kid" included several images of Lincoln and the Courthouse, including a picture of artist Peter Hurd standing in the stairwell, gazing down at the bullet holes, now surrounded by an interpretive frame.[5] This image verifies that Peter Hurd did not collaborate with John Davis to fabricate the bullet holes during Davis' tenure as the building's curator. The origin date for the bullet holes was now undeniably pushed back to at least 1941—but had John Sinclair added them to the building's interior, or was there substance to the brief mention in Burns' book? We pushed backward through time to answer this question, and another clue in the Lincoln County Historical Society archives provided that answer.

While combing the archives for previously unpublished images of the Courthouse, we discovered a picture of noted historian Maurice Garland Fulton pointing at what appears to be a bullet hole at the bottom of the famous stairwell. Indeed, it is the same bullet hole located in

Artist Peter Hurd gazing down at the purported bullet holes, 1941.
LIFE Magazine

Maurice G. Fulton pointing at the bullet hole he believed Billy the Kid left after fatally shooting James Bell. Photograph taken before 1938.
Lincoln County Historical Society

the upper left-hand portion of the wall, later framed by Sinclair. This image did not immediately generate excitement, as Fulton had served as museum curator between 1948 and 1949 and had not passed away until after Caroline Davis' tenure as curator. However, upon closer inspection, we noticed one critical detail—Garland is leaning against the north-facing wall of the stairwell, and there is no doorway in the image. This detail definitively places the image date before renovations completed by Jerome Hendron and the Museum of New Mexico between 1938 and 1939. Perhaps it was Garland himself, a friend of Burns, who showed the bullet holes to the author while conducting research for his book. This new information reinvigorated our hunt and, surprisingly, led us next to two well-known American writers and a former Territorial Governor of New Mexico.

After discovering the pre-1939 image of Maurice Fulton and the presumed bullet holes, we began pouring through newspapers and books from the period in search of any references to the elusive features. We discovered an article written in 1938 by Pulitzer Prize-winning American journalist Ernie Pyle. Best known for his coverage of troop life on the front lines during World War II, Pyle spent most of the 1930s as a "Human Interest" columnist, traveling extensively through South America, Mexico, and the American West. Pyle passed through Lincoln in the Spring of 1938, on the eve of the Museum of New Mexico's restoration of the Courthouse. In an article published in the *Albuquerque Tribune* on April 21, 1938, Pyle painted a picture of Lincoln for his readers, including details regarding the Courthouse. Specifically, Pyle

Journalist Ernie Pyle visited Lincoln in 1938, seven years before his death while covering the Battle of Okinawa.
Library of Congress

mentioned the "...hole in the wall where the Kid's bullet struck after passing through the heart of Deputy Bell."[6] Pyle's account firmly places the bullet holes in the Courthouse before the Spring of 1938, but he was not the first noted author to visit Lincoln during that decade.

Drawn by the increased public interest in Billy the Kid, pulp-fiction author Robert E. Howard toured Lincoln in June, 1935. Howard's experience must have been noteworthy as he wrote about his time in Lincoln in a letter to fellow author H.P. Lovecraft. Howard vividly described the Courthouse in the letter: "We saw the stair where Bell made his desperate break and the hole in the wall at the floor where the Kid's bullet had lodged, after tearing its way through Bell's heart."[7] With this description, courtesy of the creator of Conan the Barbarian, it was clear that Billy's mysterious bullet holes existed as early as 1935.

Moving steadily backward, we discovered that in the summer of 1933, author Leslie Traylor had visited Lincoln to tour the historic sites and interview several residents, including Yginio Salazar. Traylor wrote about his visit to Lincoln in an article for the *Frontier Times*, in July of 1936. In the article, Traylor provided this description of what he believed to be a bullet hole at the bottom of the staircase, although his conclusion differed from the report of Bell's death provided by Pat Garrett.

The hole where the bullet was embedded in the adobe wall is at the foot of the stairway, and on the far side from the top of the stairs, also it is above the shoulders of the height of an average man. We found no signs of where a bullet had caromed. If Bell, on entering to go up the stairway had been shot as he faced Billy the Kid, whether the Kid was at the top of the stairs or near the bottom, Bell would have been shot through and through, from front to back, and the bullet hole would have been a foot or more lower than it was. If Billy had shot Bell from the top of the stairs, and Bell had been about three steps from the top, then Bell's breast, or any person of average height would have been in line with Billy, and the bullet hole, in the adobe wall which is at the foot of the stair way, and on the far side in the center. So we reached the conclusion that if Bell had been shot while on the stairway, he was almost at the top of the stairs when he was killed.[8]

(L to R) Marshall Bond, Jr., Miguel Otero, Jr., Susan McSween-Barber, Marshall Bond, Sr., and his wife Amy Louise Bond, Summer 1923, White Oaks, NM
Lincoln County Historical Society

Traylor's 1933 trip to Lincoln pushed the existence of the bullet holes back nearly a decade before John Sinclair placed them under glass, but the trail did not end there. The late 1920s and 1930s saw a marked increase in visitors to New Mexico as curiosity surrounding the Lincoln County War and Billy the Kid skyrocketed. <u>The Saga of Billy the Kid</u> and King Vidor's 1930 movie, *Billy the Kid,* fueled a renewed interest in Billy and Lincoln. In the late 1920s, many community members in Lincoln began exploring the idea of preserving the town and promoting it as a heritage tourism destination. In an article published in the Albuquerque Journal in April 1927, the author shared that,

> *Tourists will be shown where Billy the Kid was besieged by an opposing faction before the kid went on his final rampage, the old ruins, the places where so many men were killed, where Billy was imprisoned, where he escaped, bullet holes in walls, the spots of desperate and bloody encounters.[9]*

There was clear evidence that the bullet holes, regardless of authenticity, were there in the Courthouse as early as 1927, two years after The Saga of Billy the Kid was copyrighted. However crucial to catapulting Billy the Kid to stardom, Walter Noble Burns' book contained countless elaborations, mistruths, and outright falsehoods. The book's troublesome retelling of Billy the Kid's life and the events surrounding the Lincoln County War encouraged numerous New Mexicans to come forward with their accountings of what had transpired. These included compatriots of Billy the Kid, such as Frank and George Coe, as well as former New Mexico Territorial Governor Miguel Otero, Jr. Born in October 1859, Otero followed in the footsteps of his father, becoming a successful businessman, politician, and the sixteenth Governor of Territorial New Mexico between 1897 and 1906. Based on personal experiences, Otero published The Real Billy the Kid; With New Light on the Lincoln County War in 1936. A commercial success, the book painted a sympathetic picture of Billy the Kid while weaving a tale filled with great locational detail. Although published in 1936, several chapters of Otero's book describe a trip the former governor took a decade earlier, in July 1926. Alongside his long-time friend Marshall Bond, Sr., Otero revisited many places he wrote about in his narrative, including a visit to the Lincoln County Courthouse. Otero recounts, "We saw the hole which was made by the bullet that pierced Bell's body."[10] The former governor also recalled his first trip to Lincoln in 1883 when he slept in the Courthouse as the guest of Deputy Sheriff James Brent. Either Otero did not recall seeing the bullet holes then or simply presumed that his readers would infer they had been there in 1883. Regardless, the bullet holes, authentic or not, were present during Otero's trip to Lincoln in the summer of 1926—proving that Walter Noble Burns based his reference to the bullet holes in his book on some level of fact and not outright fiction.

We had landed back at the beginning of our trail—Walter Noble Burns and his critical, albeit factually deficient, Saga of Billy the Kid. Burns' research for this seminal work included a lengthy trip to New Mexico in the summer of 1923. Burns' cousin, Katherine, had married New Mexico attorney and politician Thomas Jewett Mabry in 1915 after the death of Mabry's first wife, Winifred, in July 1912.[11] Katherine Burns-Mabry attended the University of New Mexico and, in 1917, became the first woman admitted to the New Mexico State Bar Association.[12] In July 1923, Katherine's cousin Walter and his wife Rose visited the Mabry family. They embarked on an ambitious trip around the state, which Walter later called "The New Mexico Expedition."[13] Burns and various

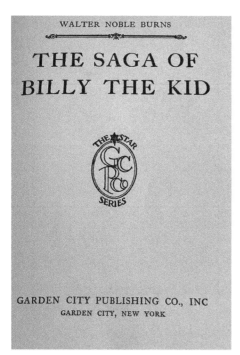

WALTER NOBLE BURNS

THE SAGA OF BILLY THE KID

THE STAR SERIES

GARDEN CITY PUBLISHING CO., INC
GARDEN CITY, NEW YORK

Published in 1926, Walter Noble Burns' book on Billy the Kid made the outlaw a household name, leading to several motion pictures and countless other re-tellings of his brief life.

members of his family toured the state for nearly two months, interviewing dozens of people associated with Billy the Kid and the Lincoln County War. Among these interviewees were Alexander McSween's widow, Susan McSween-Barber, and regulators Yginio Salazar, Frank Coe, and George Coe. Burns walked the streets of old Lincoln with those who had experienced the violence of the Lincoln County War firsthand and saw for himself the legendary bullet holes left in the wall of the Courthouse stairwell.

1923—this is where the trail ran cold. The mysterious bullet holes seemingly disappeared from the record before Walter Noble Burns' research trip to New Mexico. Between Pat Garrett's description in 1881 and the second decade of the 20th century, we could find no reference to the bullet holes in newspapers, county records, dime novels, or anywhere else. For forty years, the bullet scars seemingly disappeared from recorded history, leading to the question—did Burns fabricate the bullet holes himself while visiting Lincoln or possibly find two holes in the wall of an old building and jump to the massive conclusion that they were placed there by Billy the Kid's pistol? Historian Maurice G. Fulton certainly believed that the holes dated to the Kid's escape, and it is not clear whether he accompanied Burns during his trip to Lincoln in 1923. Fulton moved to New Mexico in 1922 to teach at the New Mexico Military Institute. He and Burns maintained a professional relationship after publishing The Saga of Billy the Kid in 1926. However, neither of the men's correspondence dates before 1926. Could Fulton have read Burns' book, leading him to discover and validate the reported bullet holes? With the evidence on hand, our search halted, leaving the authenticity of the scars on the wall in serious question. However, one more piece of evidence presented itself—ultimately breathing life back into the legend and leaving us with at least the possibility that Billy's mark was still visible on the Courthouse wall.

John Sinclair spent the entirety of his short tenure as the Courthouse Museum's first curator researching the Lincoln County War and interviewing dozens of residents. His efforts provided valuable understanding into the lives of Lincoln's everyday citizens during the region's period of unrivaled violence and the final clue in our attempt to shine a light on the mysterious bullet holes. In an article he published in the July 28, 1940 edition of the *Santa Fe New Mexican,* Sinclair described his ongoing friendship with Lincoln resident Francisco Gomez. Born in 1853, Gomez served as Lincoln County Probate Judge and helped make adobe bricks for the construction of the Lincoln County Courthouse in 1873. Sinclair's conversations with Gomez provided unique insight into the building's construction, and in one tour of the structure, Gomez pointed out to Sinclair, "...where the dying man (James Bell) had placed his bloody hands on the wall beside the bullet holes and the prints of which could be seen for many years."[14] Gomez's casual statement to Sinclair is the only known corroboration that Billy the Kid left his permanent mark on the stairwell wall. Gomez worked in the building for more than three decades as both Probate Judge and Justice of the Peace, and his assertion that the marks date to that fateful day in April 1881 is the closest thing we have to confirmation of their authenticity. However, this final bit of evidence we discovered was largely circumstantial and anecdotal. Accepting Mr. Gomez at his word would confirm that the bullet holes are remnants of Billy the Kid's violent escape.

All historical evidence aside, there is still the issue of physics and the laws of nature. Garrett likely based his published description of Bell's death on the official coroner's inquest, which does not support the contention that the fatal bullet lodged in the west wall. Garrett stated that the deadly bullet ricocheted off the wall to Bell's right, passed through his torso, and embedded itself in the wall to his left. This places the bullet's final resting place somewhere along the south wall of the stairwell and not at the bottom of the landing. If Garrett's account is accurate, then Burns and Fulton's assertion that the hole at the bottom of the stairwell

Former Lincoln County Probate Judge and Justice of the Peace, Francisco Gomez with Ed Penfield. Photograph taken by John Sinclair, c.1940
Lincoln County Historical Society

originated from the fatal bullet is simply impossible—but what about the other shot Billy possibly fired?

On the day of Billy's escape, Gottfried Gauss said he heard two gunshots from within the Courthouse. If this is to be believed, then one of those two shots did not strike Bell and could have ended up at the bottom of the landing. The location of the bullet scar at the bottom of the stairs is also problematic regarding Burns and Fulton's claims. If Billy indeed shot Bell at the bottom of the stairs while he himself stood at the top of the landing, then the bullet would have been traveling along a downward trajectory and most likely buried itself much lower than where the mark is now. However, bullets traveling through the human body are often unpredictable, and there are countless documented cases where a bullet changes direction once hitting a person and exits from an unlikely location and along a different path from its original trajectory.

While we did not necessarily uncover irrefutable evidence either discrediting or confirming the authenticity of the bullet holes, we were able to establish that multiple well-respected authors, politicians, and historians saw what they believed to be physical evidence left over from the last escape of Billy the Kid before 1950 and that at least one person alive at the time of his escape corroborated their veracity—albeit nearly six decades after the event. The likelihood that Billy the Kid created the bullet scar at the bottom of the stairs is questionable at best, and even if it was, the probability that it was from the fatal shot that killed James Bell is even more implausible. For now, the legend of Billy the Kid's bullet holes lives on, along with his mythical status among personas of the American West and that of the building he has made so famous.

Tim Roberts and Billy Roberts
Lincoln, New Mexico

PART I

THE HOUSE

INTRODUCTION

Beyond a doubt, Billy the Kid is the most internationally recognizable character in American Western history. Countless authors and artists have spent their entire careers studying and memorializing this man who most likely died before his twenty-second birthday. At the epicenter of this international cult of personality stands the tiny town of Lincoln, New Mexico. Since Billy died in 1881, millions of visitors have made the pilgrimage to Lincoln, New Mexico, to follow an American legend's footsteps. More specifically, they travel to see the building from which the famed outlaw made his final violent escape on April 28, 1881. Standing at the western edge of Lincoln looms a massive edifice, noticeably out of place among the other, more modest territorial-style structures spread throughout the town. Now known as the Historic Lincoln County Courthouse, this building sits squarely at the core of both the story of Billy the Kid and how Lincoln's citizens saved their town from destruction—creating, in the process, the most well-preserved frontier town in the American West.

Seventy-Seven days after his escape, Pat Garrett ended Billy's life in Fort Sumner, but the young man's legend continued to grow beyond what anyone could imagine. Today, tens of thousands of people visit Lincoln, New Mexico, many looking to walk in Billy's footsteps. Lincoln's unparalleled historical integrity transports visitors back to a period when the West was wild. Lincoln is a town frozen in time, preserved for future generations through the efforts of many who believed it worthy of saving. Billy the Kid did not understand how his escape from the Lincoln County Courthouse would impact future generations. Still, it set in motion a movement to save the historic building—and eventually the town of Lincoln.

While Billy the Kid undoubtedly put the Historic Lincoln County Courthouse on the map, the building's fascinating history extends far beyond that fateful day in April 1881. Constructed by *L.G. Murphy and Company* in 1874, the building served as the firm's headquarters during the height of its power. From the second-floor balcony, L.G. Murphy, James Dolan, John Riley, and their associates ruled over an empire of corruption—amassing fortunes at the expense of the region's citizens. The firm's rise, however, did not survive the bloody and violent Lincoln County War, and its financial stranglehold on the region collapsed. Mounting debts forced James Dolan and John Riley to sell their keystone asset, leaving the future of the building uncertain. Fortunately, the growing population of Lincoln County needed a new seat of political and legal power and, in 1880, the County of Lincoln purchased the structure, converting the former mercantile into the county's first permanent Courthouse.

For the next three decades, the building stood as a bastion of law and order in the region, housing local government offices, dispensing justice from the county courtroom and gallows, and confining the region's criminals in the adjacent jail. For a time, the town of Lincoln flourished as the county seat, but other nearby towns began expanding themselves, eventually surpassing Lincoln in population and importance. As New Mexico's Territorial period came to a close, the citizens of Lincoln County voted to move the county seat to nearby Carrizozo. Although a bitter fight over the decision ensued, Carrizozo prevailed, and the county abandoned the Courthouse in Lincoln for several years. The community repurposed the Courthouse as a school, and the structure briefly served Lincoln's students, but when the county constructed a new permanent schoolhouse in 1920, they abandoned the building entirely. The Courthouse slowly fell into disrepair and ruin for more than a decade, hosting only the occasional tourist interested in seeing where Billy the Kid had made his famous last escape. By 1936, the building was in danger of collapsing, and county officials discussed the possibility of demolishing the structure, once and for all. Thankfully, a dedicated group of concerned citizens recognized the structure's significance and successfully saved the old building from demolition by working with the

Museum of New Mexico and the Works Progress Administration. For more than a year, workers endeavored to restore the building, and in 1939, the Courthouse reopened as a state-operated museum. The successful preservation of the Courthouse paved the way for more projects in the historic hamlet of Lincoln, serving as a model for expanded efforts to preserve the town, and ultimately leading to the community's designation as a National Historic Landmark and the establishment of a local preservation ordinance.

The story of the Courthouse is more than just the tale of a physical building, and certainly extends well beyond its brief association with Billy the Kid. The structure's history is a chronicle of the men who built it, the community it served, and the development of the American Southwest. To understand and appreciate the historical significance of the Historic Lincoln County Courthouse, it is necessary to look beyond the building's physical appearance and toward how its very existence fits into the story of Lincoln, the Territory of New Mexico, and the context of the American West. *L.G. Murphy and Company* did not break ground on the building until 1873, but the idea behind the building started long before then. In many ways, the structure represents the culmination of years of non-native expansion into the American Southwest, significant shifts in who held power over the region, and a realization of the American ideal of *Manifest Destiny*.

As important as the building's beginnings are, the tale of its preservation is an equally critical story. The recognition of the structure's significance and the efforts by so many to restore and open it to the public, represents one of the earliest attempts by the State of New Mexico to use public funding for the purpose of historic preservation. Nearly nine decades later, heritage tourism continues to serve as a major contributor to the economy of New Mexico, with millions of visitors every year traveling to the *Land of Enchantment* to experience its multi-cultural history and the authenticity of its historic landscape. At the center of this continually growing movement, stands the Historic Lincoln County Courthouse, a testament to the foresight of state leaders and a reminder that the understanding and preservation of our complex collective past, is a critical component of how we move forward as a community, as a state, and as a nation.

CHAPTER ONE
THE MAKING OF THE SOUTHWEST

Recent discoveries of fossilized footprints at White Sands National Park place the earliest humans in New Mexico, arriving between sixteen and twenty-three thousand years ago. Between that time and around five hundred BCE, various hunter and gatherer cultures survived by hunting big game across the region, specifically the eastern plains, where large herds of buffalo and mammoths gathered to graze on the edge of the Great Plains. As agricultural techniques advanced, many indigenous peoples established more permanent settlements along large rivers, including the Rio Grande, Rio Pecos, Rio Bonito, and Rio Ruidoso. During this time, members of the nomadic Athabaskan culture migrated into the southwest, including ancestors of the Apache and Navajo people.[1]

In 1539, less than fifty years after Christopher Columbus first visited the Caribbean, Vázquez de Coronado, Governor of the Kingdom of Nueva Galicia in New Spain, ordered Friar Marcos de Niza to explore modern-day New Mexico and Arizona. Upon his return, de Niza regaled Coronado and Viceroy of New Spain, Antonio de Mendoza, with tales of a city built entirely of gold called Cíbola. The following year, Coronado and Mendoza planned and funded a large expedition into the region. Coronado and his men spent nearly two fruitless years roaming from the modern Arizona/New Mexico border to as far east as Oklahoma and Texas. During their travels in Eastern New Mexico and West

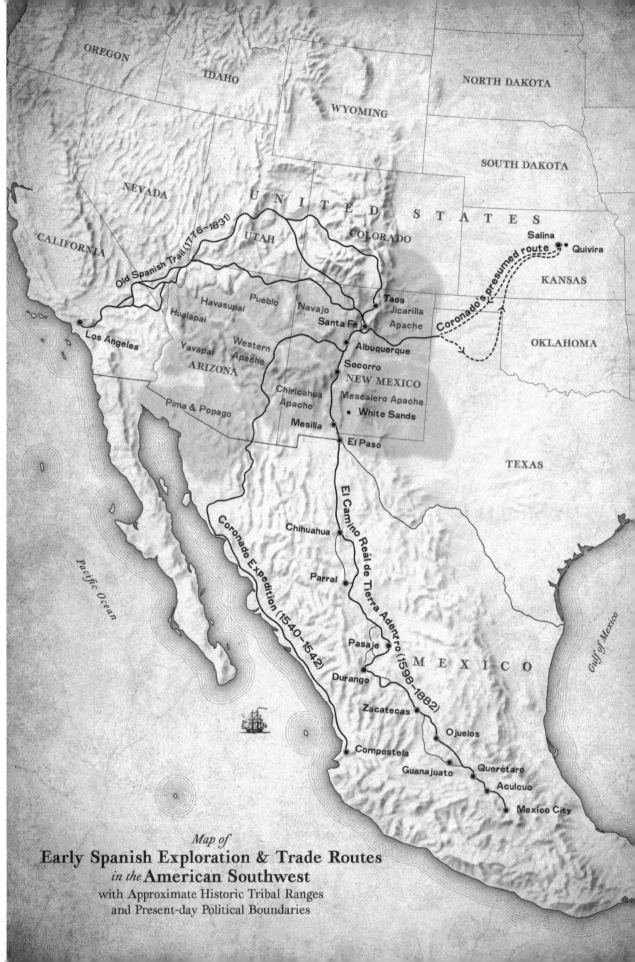

Map of
Early Spanish Exploration & Trade Routes
in the **American Southwest**
with Approximate Historic Tribal Ranges
and Present-day Political Boundaries

Texas, Coronado's expedition encountered a group of Native Americans, naming them *Querechos*. Later Spanish colonizers would call these nomadic hunters the Mescalero Apache.

Coronado's search for Cibola led him to financial ruin, and the Spanish did not send another major expedition north until 1598. That year, Juan de Oñate y Salazar traveled north from Mexico, established a permanent settlement along the Rio Grande at San Juan de Los Caballeros, and accepted an appointment as the first Spanish Colonial Governor of the Province of *Santa Fe de Nuevo México*. In 1610, the Spanish moved the provincial capital to Santa Fe, maintaining control of the region for seventy years through a system based upon the enslavement of the native Puebloan peoples. In 1680, the Pueblos united under the leadership of a Tewa religious leader from Ohkay Owingeh Pueblo named Po'pay. The Puebloans revolted under Po'pay's leadership and forced the Spanish to completely abandon New Mexico and flee south back to New Spain. Twelve years later, the Spanish returned to New Mexico under the leadership of Diego de Vargas and marched back into Santa Fe unopposed. De Vargas promised the Puebloans peace and amnesty for their actions during the revolt. All but a few isolated Pueblos, far to the west of the Rio Grande, pledged allegiance to the King of Spain.

With their colony reestablished, Spanish officials resumed sending wagon trains filled with goods south along the El Camino Real de Tierra Adentro (Royal Road of the Interior) that extended from points north of Santa Fe to Mexico City. The El Camino Real largely followed the Rio Grande in New Mexico, and settlers established new villages along its banks. These included La Villa de Albuquerque, Socorro, and Mesilla.[2]

Following America's War of Independence, the new government of the United States began eying expansion into the western portions of North America. In 1803, the United States finalized the Louisiana Purchase with the Republic of France, expanding their holdings across the continent by more than eight hundred thousand square miles. Included in this deal was the area now known as the Texas panhandle and portions of northeastern New Mexico and southeastern Colorado. Spain claimed these lands as their own and argued that France had no right to sell them. Tensions between the United States and Spain increased after the Louisiana Purchase, and the Spanish government restricted American access to the Santa Fe Trail. Those who attempted to move goods between the United States and New Spain were often arrested and sent to Mexico City for trial and imprisonment. In 1819, the United States and Spain signed the Adams–Onís Treaty, which officially ceded Florida to the United States and established a western border with New Spain that excluded the previously contested areas in New Mexico and Colorado. During this time, Spain was also struggling with internal conflicts in New Spain, and in August 1821, it officially recognized Mexico's independence after signing the Treaty of Córdoba.

With this transition in power came new economic opportunities for those willing to take the risk of traveling between the Mississippi River Valley and the Southwest. Native Americans, French trappers, and American merchants constructed an informal trade route connecting America to New Mexico through modern Missouri, Kansas, Texas, and Colorado. This trade trail terminated at Santa Fe, where it extended all the way south to Mexico City via the El Camino Real. The Santa Fe Trail played a critical role in the expansion of the newest political player in the region—the United States of America. The regime change in New Mexico immediately affected commerce along the Santa Fe Trail, as the new Mexican government welcomed traders from the United States with open arms. One month after Mexico gained independence, American trader William Becknell departed Franklin, Missouri, for Santa Fe. When Becknell arrived in New Mexico, he discovered a new government and a positive reception. By 1825, merchants from the United States and Mexico were trading goods along the route, including settlements south of Santa Fe along the Rio Grande River.

In 1845, columnist John O'Sullivan penned a widely circulated essay, "Annexation." In the article, O'Sullivan argued in favor of America annexing the Republic of Texas. Perhaps inspired by the successful Texan revolt against Mexico a decade earlier, O'Sullivan coined a new term, *Manifest Destiny*—his assertion that the United States was destined to spread across the entire North American continent.[3] O'Sullivan's idea spread like wildfire across the nation, and later that year, the United States absorbed Texas into the republic. Mexico disputed the United States' right to annex Texas leading to war breaking out in 1846. At the outset of the war, United States Secretary of War William L. Marcy authorized General Stephen Watts Kearny to raise an *Army of the West* to invade Mexico's territories west of Texas, including New Mexico and California. With more than sixteen hundred men under his command, Kearny departed Fort Leavenworth, Kansas, in June 1846. The *Army of the West* traveled southwest along the Santa Fe Trail, arriving on the outskirts of Santa Fe on August 18th, 1846. Kearny sent word to New Mexican governor Manuel Armijo that the United States intended to take possession of the territory and marched his army triumphantly into Santa Fe without firing a single shot. Kearny estab-

Map of
U.S. Territorial Acquisition
in the American Southwest

WYOMING

NEBRASKA

IOWA

Denver

COLORADO

Fort Leavenworth

Fra

Abilene   Kansas City

Ellsworth   Independence

KANSAS

MISSOUR

Pueblo   Bent's Fort

Dodge City

Arkansas River

Raton
Taos

INDIAN

Santa Fe   Fort Union
Las Vegas

Canadian River

Albuquerque

Amarillo

Fort Smith

NEW MEXICO

Fort Sumner

TERRITORY

ARKANSA

Red River

Pecos River

Fort Stanton

Roswell

TEXAS

Fort Worth

El Paso

Colorado River

Rio Grande

Austin

San Antonio

Houston

MEXICO

Rio Grande

Galveston

Laredo

Corpus Christi

Gulf of Mexico

Brownsville

Map of
Major Historic Overland Routes
of the **American Southwest**

—— Chisholm Trail (1867–1876)
—— Goodnight-Loving Trail (1866–1884)
—— Santa Fe Trail (1821–1880)

lished a joint civil-military government in New Mexico, appointing merchant Charles Bent as Civilian Governor and Colonel Sterling Price as Military Governor. Kearny then continued with three-hundred men to California, but a group of Mexicans and Puebloans organized a revolt in his absence. These insurgents murdered Charles Bent at his home in Taos but failed to retake Santa Fe, facing a crushing defeat by Price and his army at the Battle of Cañada.

On February 2, 1848, the United States and Mexico signed the Treaty of Guadalupe-Hidalgo, officially ending the Mexican American War and ceding the United States the land that would become New Mexico. Almost immediately, enterprising pioneers began pouring into the region, searching for opportunity and fortune. New Mexico sat on the frontier's edge, far away from the watchful eye of Washington, D.C. In the region surrounding Sierra Blanca Peak, the Mescalero Apache people had lived in relative isolation, away from non-native settlers, since Spanish explorers first set foot in New Mexico. The Spanish and Mexican governments restricted their citizens from settling in the region, but this policy changed suddenly following the American annexation of New Mexico. The recently signed Treaty of Guadalupe-Hidalgo guaranteed settlers the right to move into the entirety of the Southwest and promised protection from "Indian Depredations."[4] For the first time, non-natives sought to establish permanent settlements in the Rio Bonito Valley, located one-hundred miles east of the Rio Grande River. In 1852, Colonel Edwin Vose Sumner, commander of the Army's Department of New Mexico and acting Superintendent of Indian Affairs John Greiner, signed a treaty with representatives of numerous Apache bands, including the

"Conquest of New Mexico", an engraving of General Kearney proclaiming New Mexico part of the United States, Plaza, Las Vegas, New Mexico, 15 August 1846.
Public Domain

Mescalero Apache. In return for a guarantee of peace, the Army ensured the Mescalero Apache that their ancestral homeland in the Sacramento Mountains of Southeastern New Mexico would be off-limits to non-native settlers.[5] However, the Army's promise to the Mescalero Apache people contradicted the guarantees of the Treaty of Guadalupe-Hidalgo. Within a few short years, Hispanic and Anglo settlers began arriving in the region, including the fertile Rio Bonito Valley in the shadow of the Mescalero Apache people's most sacred mountain, Sierra Blanca.

In the winter of 1855, Major James Carleton and the 1st U.S. Dragoons assisted in constructing and opening a wagon road from Albuquerque to the Rio Bonito Valley—further encouraging non-native settlement in the region.[6] This influx of new settlers led to tensions with the native population of the area, and Mescalero Apache raids on settlements increased significantly. In response, Brigadier General John Garland, commander of the Department of New Mexico, ordered members of the 1st U.S. Dragoons to travel north from Fort Fillmore to locate the Mescalero Apache responsible for disrupting settlement attempts along the Rio Bonito. On January 18th, 1855, Company "B" of the 1st Dragoons engaged with a small group of Mescalero along the Rio Peñasco. While following a trail from an abandoned camp, a group of Mescalero ambushed Captain Henry Whiting Stanton and a small detachment of men, killing Captain Stanton during the skirmish.[7] The escalating violence between settlers and the Mescalero Apache encouraged the War Department to establish a permanent post in the region. In March 1855, Lieutenant Colonel Dixon Miles marched three hundred men of the 3rd U.S. Infantry, 8th U.S. Infantry, and 1st U.S. Dragoons into the heart of the Mescalero Apache homeland to establish a new fort.

On April 11th, 1855, Lieutenant Colonel Miles and Major James Carleton initially chose a location in the Rio Hondo Valley, reporting from the proposed site, "The valley is rich and fit for cultivation all the way. And hence upwards towards the White Mountains, where the Bonito and Ruidoso have their sources, the Bonito River bottom is very rich, at least for more than twenty miles which I have examined."[8]

Although this first location met all of the necessary requirements for the new post, Dixon and Carleton ultimately chose a location sixteen miles northwest, along the upper Rio Bonito. The Army officially established the new post on May 4th, 1855, naming it in honor of the recently killed Captain Henry Stanton.[9] With a permanent Army presence in the heart of the Mescalero Apache homeland, Apache leaders Cadete and Barranquito endeavored to develop friendly relations with the U.S. Government. Dr. Michael Steck, an

The First official monthly post return from Fort Stanton (May 1855), recording its establishment by members of the 1st Dragoons, 3rd Infantry, 8th Infantry, and New Mexico Volunteers
National Archives and Records Administration

Indian Agent for the Mescalero Apache, assisted in negotiating between the government and the tribe, brokering a meeting at Fort Thorn between Apache leaders and Territorial Governor David Meriwether in the summer of 1855. In return for an end to hostilities, Meriwether promised a reservation for the Mescalero Apache along the Rio Ruidoso and an Indian Agency at Fort Stanton. Congress never ratified this treaty, but for the time being, the Mescalero Apache ceased raids on settlements along the Rio Bonito.

With the Army now permanently garrisoned in the region and a tenuous peace brokered with the Mescalero Apache, families from the Rio Grande Valley began flooding into the area. By the end of 1855, newcomers had established several small homesteads and *Placitas* adjacent to the river, including a growing village called *La Placita del Rio Bonito*—located eight miles east of Fort Stanton.[10] Settlement in the region expanded rapidly, and in 1869, the Territorial Representative voted to carve out a new county from Socorro County. The legislature recommended it be called Baca County in honor of Civil War Veteran and territorial legislator Saturnino Baca. Although humbled by the sentiment, Baca suggested the legislature name the county in honor of the late President Abraham Lincoln. Following this decision, citizens selected *La Placita del Rio Bonito* as the county seat, renaming it Lincoln.

CHAPTER TWO
THE RISE OF THE HOUSE OF MURPHY

When the American Civil War erupted in 1861, the United States Army sent troops into New Mexico to protect the territory from Confederate invasion. Many who came to New Mexico to secure the region elected to stay after the war to make new lives for themselves. Two of these new settlers included Army veterans Lawrence G. Murphy and Emil Fritz.

Born in County Wexford, Ireland, L.G. Murphy immigrated to the United States in 1851 and enlisted in the 5th U.S. Infantry at Buffalo, New York, in July of the same year.[1] Murphy served in Texas, Florida, and Utah, before arriving in New Mexico and mustering out of the Army on April 26, 1861, just two weeks before the U.S. Civil War began. The ambitious Irishman did not remain a civilian for very long, accepting a commission as a First Lieutenant in the 1st Regiment of the New Mexico Volunteer Cavalry on July 17, 1861.[2] Murphy's first trip to Lincoln County occurred in October 1862, when he traveled with his company to reoccupy Fort Stanton. Federal troops had abandoned the post in the face of advancing Confederate forces in August 1861, setting fire to the fort's buildings as they marched north. A fortuitous rainstorm extinguished the flames before they destroyed the post, and Confederate troops briefly occupied the remains before fleeing from New Mexico following the March 1862 battle of Glorieta Pass.

In 1863, Murphy grew tired of his role as a quartermaster and recruiter for the regiment and requested permission to resign his commission and join the war effort back east. His commanding officer, Colonel Christopher "Kit" Carson, convinced Murphy not

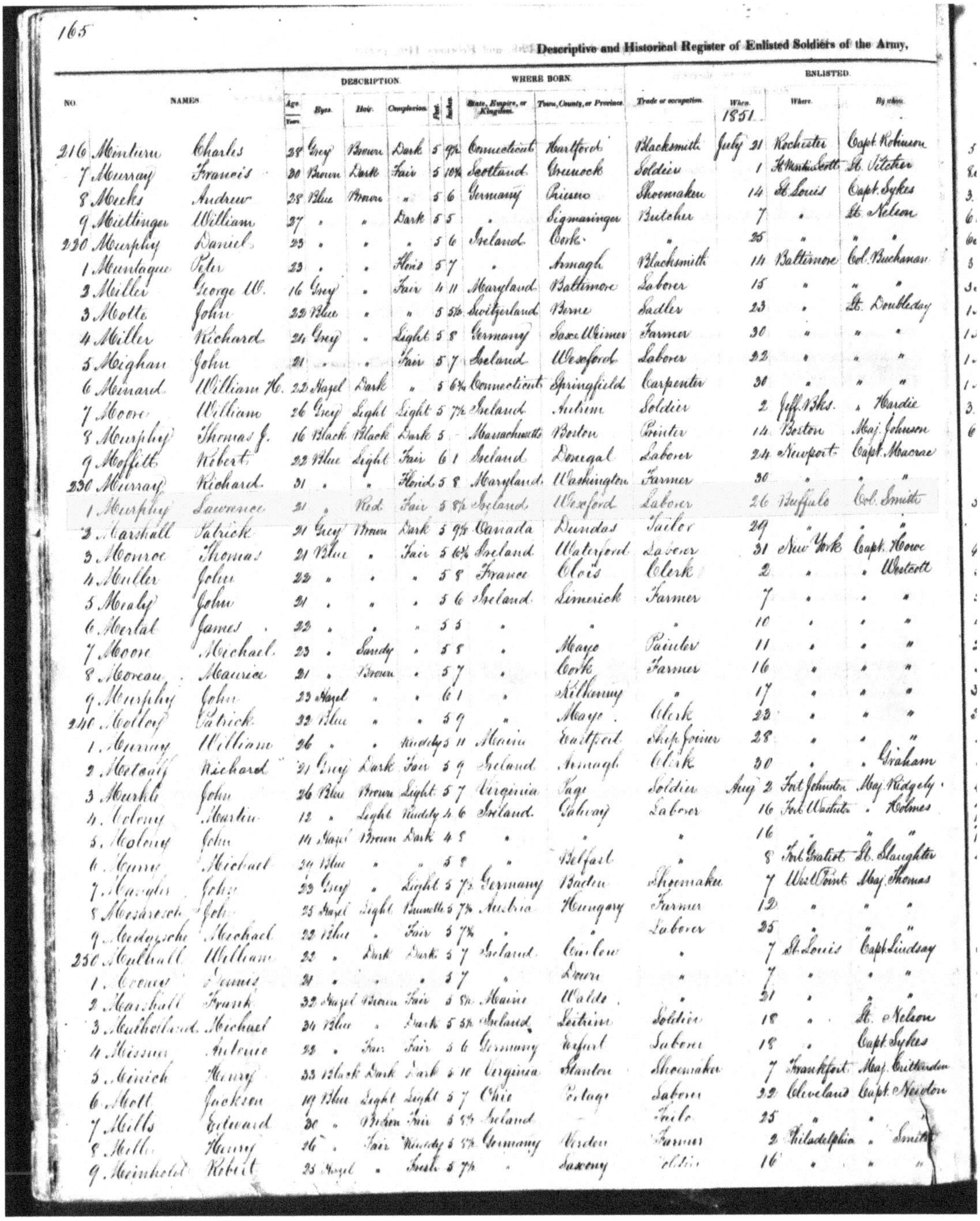

Descriptive and Historical Register of Enlisted Soldiers of the Army,

NO.	NAMES		Age Years	Eyes	Hair	Complexion	Feet	Inches	State, Empire, or Kingdom	Town, County, or Province	Trade or occupation	When 1851	Where	By whom	
216	Minturn	Charles	28	Grey	Brown	Dark	5	9½	Connecticut	Hartford	Blacksmith	July 31	Rochester	Capt. Robinson	5
7	Murray	Francis	30	Brown	Dark	Fair	5	10½	Scotland	Greenock	Soldier	1	Jt. Montn Scott	Jt. Viteher	8
8	Meeks	Andrew	28	Blue	Brown	"	5	6	Germany	Greeno	Shoemaker	14	St. Louis	Capt. Sykes	3
9	Mietinger	William	37	"	"	Dark	5	5	Sigmaringen		Butcher	7	"	Jt. Nelson	6
230	Murphy	Daniel	23	"	"	"	5	6	Ireland	Cork		25	"		6
1	Montague	Peter	23	"	"	Flond	5	7		Armagh	Blacksmith	14	Baltimore	Col. Buchanan	3
2	Miller	George W.	16	Grey	"	Fair	4	11	Maryland	Baltimore	Laborer	15	"		3
3	Motte	John	22	Blue	"	"	5	5½	Switzerland	Berne	Sadler	23	"	Jt. Doubleday	1
4	Miller	Richard	21	Grey	"	Light	5	8	Germany	Saxe Weimer	Farmer	30	"	"	1
5	Meighan	John	21	"	"	Fair	5	7	Ireland	Wexford	Laborer	22	"	"	1
6	Menard	William H.	22	Hazel	Dark	"	5	6½	Connecticut	Springfield	Carpenter	30	"	"	1
7	Moore	William	26	Grey	Light	Light	5	7½	Ireland	Antrim	Soldier	2	Jeff. Bks.	" Hardie	3
8	Murphy	Thomas J.	16	Black	Black	Dark	5		Massachusetts	Boston	Printer	14	Boston	Maj. Johnson	6
9	Moffitt	Robert	22	Blue	Light	Fair	6	1	Ireland	Donegal	Laborer	24	Newport	Capt. Macrae	
230	Murray	Richard	31	"	"	Flond	5	8	Maryland	Washington	Farmer	30	"		5
1	Murphy	Lawrence	21	"	Red	Fair	5	8½	Ireland	Wexford	Laborer	26	Buffalo	Col. Smith	5
2	Marshall	Patrick	21	Grey	Brown	Dark	5	9½	Canada	Dundas	Tailor	29	"		4
3	Monroe	Thomas	21	Blue	"	Fair	5	6½	Ireland	Waterford	Laborer	31	New York	Capt. Moore	4
4	Muller	John	22	"	"	"	5	8	France	Clois	Clerk	2	"	Westcott	
5	Mealy	John	21	"	"	"	5	6	Ireland	Limerick	Farmer	7	"	"	
6	Mertal	James	22	"	"	"	5	5	"			10	"	"	
7	Moore	Michael	23	"	Sandy	"	5	8	"	Mayo	Painter	11	"	"	
8	Moreau	Maurice	21	"	Brown	"	5	7	"	Cork	Farmer	16	"	"	
9	Murphy	John	23	Hazel	"	"	6	1	"	Kilkenny		17	"	"	3
248	Molloy	Patrick	22	Blue	"	"	5	9	"	Mayo	Clerk	23	"	"	
1	Murry	William	26	"	"	Ruddy	5	11	Maine	Eastport	Ship Joiner	28	"	"	
2	Metcalf	Richard	21	Grey	Dark	Fair	5	9	Ireland	Armagh	Clerk	30	"	Graham	
3	Markle	John	26	Blue	Brown	Light	5	7	Virginia	Sage	Soldier	Aug 2	Fort Johnston	Maj. Ridgely	
4	Colony	Martin	12	"	Light	Ruddy	4	6	Ireland	Galway	Laborer	16	Fort Washita	Holmes	
5	Molony	John	14	Hazel	Brown	Dark	4	8	"			16	"	"	
6	Murry	Michael	24	Blue	"	"	5	8		Belfast	Shoemaker	8	Fort Gratiot	Jt. Slaughter	
7	Laube	John	23	Grey	"	Light	5	7½	Germany	Baden	Shoemaker	7	West Point	Maj. Thomas	
8	Moravek	John	23	Hazel	Light	Thumb	5	7½	Austria	Hungary	Farmer	12	"	"	
9	Medyszchi	Michael	22	Blue	"	Fair	5	7½			Laborer	25	"	"	
250	Mulhall	William	22	"	Dark	Dark	5	7	Ireland	Carlow		7	St. Louis	Capt. Lindsay	
1	Coone	James	21	"	"	"	5	7	"	Down		7	"	"	
2	Marshall	Frank	32	Hazel	Brown	Fair	5	8½	Maine	Waldo		31	"	"	
3	Sutherland	Michael	34	Blue	"	Dark	5	5½	Ireland	Leitrim	Soldier	18	"	Jt. Nelson	
4	Missner	Antonio	22	"	Fair	Fair	5	6	Germany	Erfurt	Laborer	18	"	Capt. Sykes	
5	Minich	Henry	33	Black	Dark	Dark	5	10	Virginia	Stanton	Shoemaker	7	Frankfort	Maj. Cuthenden	
6	Mott	Jackson	19	Blue	Light	Light	5	7	Ohio	Portage	Laborer	22	Cleveland	Capt. Newton	
7	Mills	Edward	30	Brown	Fair	"	5	5½	Ireland		Tailor	25	"	"	
8	Molle	Henry	26	"	Fair	Ruddy	5	5½	Germany	Verden	Farmer	2	Philadelphia	Smith	
9	Meinhold	Robert	25	Hazel	"	Fresh	5	7½		Saxony	Soldier	16	"	"	

Lawrence Gustave Murphy's Army Enlistment Record. Murphy enlisted at Buffalo, New York on July 26, 1851 in Co. "F" of the 5th Infantry. He was 21 years old and described as having a "fair" complexion, red hair, and being 5'8.5" tall.

National Archives and Records Administration

to leave New Mexico and instead join him in his campaign against the Navajo. Murphy distinguished himself during this punitive expedition into western New Mexico and Eastern Arizona, serving as "Kit" Carson's Acting Assistant Adjutant General and gaining the respect of the famous frontiersman and soldier.[3] Following the Navajo Campaign, recently promoted Captain Lawrence Murphy took command of Company G, First New Mexico Cavalry, stationed at Fort Sumner. Murphy's unit assisted with securing and policing the nearly nine-thousand Navajo and Mescalero Apache prisoners confined at the Bosque Redondo Indian Reservation, headquartered at Fort Sumner.[4] In October 1865, the Army promoted Murphy to Major and appointed him as acting agent for the Mescalero Apache at the Bosque Redondo reservation.[5]

In November 1865, more than three hundred and fifty Mescalero Apache at Fort Sumner escaped from the Bosque Redondo Reservation and scattered across eastern New Mexico and Western Texas. Major Murphy led the expedition to recapture the prisoners but failed in his attempts to locate the escapees. With no Mescalero Apache to serve as their agent, the Army sent Major Murphy to Fort Stanton in April 1865, where he relieved his friend Emil Fritz as the post's commander. In this role, Murphy built relationships with Mescalero Apache leaders that served him well in later years.[6]

Emil Christian Adolf Fritz during his Civil War service, c.1864
Lincoln County Historical Society

A native of Ludwigsburg, Germany, Emil Christian Adolf Fritz immigrated to America in 1850 at eighteen.[7] Like his future business partner, L.G. Murphy, Emil Fritz enlisted in the U.S. Army—entering service with Company "K" of the 1st Dragoons in March 1851.[8] During his first ten years of service, Fritz served throughout the West, including New Mexico. In June 1854, Fritz and Company "K" rode into Santa

Fe, two months before the Army moved the regimental headquarters for the 1st Dragoons to Fort Union, New Mexico Territory.[9] Fritz's company deployed to Fort Craig and Fort Stanton and engaged in skirmishes with Mescalero and Chiricahua Apache. In 1856, Fritz moved west with his regiment to Fort Tejon, California, where his company participated in campaigns against the Mojave, Utes, and Paiutes during the years leading up to the American Civil War.[10] Fritz's commander in Company "K" during his time in New Mexico and California was James Henry Carleton, future commander of the Department of New Mexico. Three months before the American Civil War began, Emil Fritz mustered out of the Army, briefly working in the California gold mines before being commissioned a Captain in Com-

Brigadier general James Henry Carleton, c.1865
Library of Congress

pany "B" of the newly formed 1st California Volunteer Cavalry.[11] In 1862, Fritz traveled to New Mexico with Carleton and the "California Column." Fritz's service in New Mexico took him to posts across the entire territory, including Fort Wingate, Fort Sumner, Fort West, Fort McRae, Fort Fillmore, and Fort Stanton. At Fort Stanton, Brevet Lieutenant Colonel Fritz served as post commander between October 1865 and April 1866.[12] Lieutenant Colonel Fritz mustered out of the Army for a final time on September 16, 1866, following a brief tenure as the post commander in Albuquerque.[13]

After the Confederacy abandoned its attempt to invade New Mexico in 1862, General James Carleton turned the attention of the Army toward the native populations of the region. Murphy and Fritz took part in the campaigns against the Mescalero Apache and Navajo between 1862 and 1863 and found themselves stationed at Fort Sumner and Fort Stanton. Fort Sumner sat at the center of the newly created Bosque Redondo Reservation, where Carleton planned to resettle the Navajo and Mescalero Apache permanently. The

Map of
**Southeastern
New Mexico**
circa **1879**

first member of the Mescalero Apache tribe arrived at the new reservation in the winter of 1862, escorted from Fort Stanton by members of the 1st New Mexico Volunteers.

Eventually, the Army detained more than five-hundred Mescalero Apache at the Bosque Redondo Reservation, while the number of Navajo peaked at about eighty-five hundred. While at these posts, Murphy and Fritz learned firsthand how to prosper in New Mexico's environment of corruption—primarily through exploiting government contracts associated with the Indian Agencies. As career Army veterans, Murphy and Fritz understood the inner workings of the Government's supply chain and logistics and saw the opportunity for profit in the suffering of the Mescalero Apache and Navajo. Murphy established a personal relationship with many Mescalero Apache leaders, including Chief Cadette, while acting Indian Agent for the Mescalero Apache between June and October 1865.[14] Murphy and Fritz also worked directly with the Army's post trader at Fort Sumner, Joseph Alexander LaRue. LaRue held a license to sell goods to the soldiers stationed at the post not available through the Army's commissary. [15] The position of post trader was lucrative, to say the least, with one newspaper editorial of the time describing the coveted position as "nothing more or less than a licensed institution to fleece the soldier."[16]

LaRue's time at Fort Sumner was not without incident, and the Army accused him on at least two occasions of selling goods belonging to the Navajo and Apache. In January 1866, L.G. Murphy and other officers and friends of LaRue recommended the Army renew his contract as a post trader when his current term ended in March. Despite the endorsement of his cronies, Oscar Brown, former Colonel of the 1st Regiment of California Volunteer Cavalry, received the appointment.[17] Little did the Army know that LaRue was already planning for a move south and new business opportunities at Fort Stanton.

Both L.G. Murphy and Emil Fritz ended their military careers after serving briefly as the commander of Fort Stanton. During these last months of service, both men looked toward the future, contemplating combining their knowledge of the Army supply chain with their growing relations with Mescalero leaders. In May 1866, Fritz, now commander of Fort Stanton, issued an executive order at Fort Stanton, convening a council of administration to recommend a new post-sutler. An earlier commission of officers determined that the current post trader, Lucien B. Maxwell, had failed in his duties and, therefore, should not continue in his position. Appointed by the War Department in 1863, Maxwell had never stepped foot at Fort Stanton during his tenure, and the post's officers now looked towards one of their own to fill the position. On May 3, 1866, the council of four officers, including Captain Paul Dowlin and Captain William Brady, recommended that the army grant L.G. Murphy the position of post-sutler. Murphy sent letters to the War Department in Washington, leveraging his nearly two decades of military service and understanding of the military supply chain. Murphy's pleas paid off, and the Army appointed him Post Trader in 1866.

It is unclear whether Murphy, Fritz, and LaRue established their new firm of *L.G. Murphy and Company* before or after Murphy's appointment as Post Trader. What is certain is that Fritz transitioned directly into his ownership role with the firm after mustering

Joseph A. LaRue's involvement in the firm of L.G. Murphy & Company was previously unknown and it is still not clear exactly what role he played in the business. Born in 1831 in Monmouth County , New Jersey, LaRue immigrated to New Mexico in the 1850s working in both the mercantile and cattle businesses.

It is uncertain why LaRue, Murphy, and Fritz parted ways in 1869, but he remained involved in Lincoln County business and politics until moving to Las Vegas, NM about 1885. During the early 1880s, LaRue owned and operated a dry goods store in the building originally built and owned by John H.. Tunstall
Lincoln County Historical Society

DISSOLUTION NOTICE.

The copartnership heretofore existing between the undersigned at Fort Stanton, New Mexico, is this day dissolved by mutual consent, J. A. LaRue withdrawing from the firm. All debts due to or from the firm will be collected and paid by L G. Murphy & Co
J. A. LARUE.
LAWce G. MURPHY.
EMIL FRITZ.

☞ The business will be continued as heretofore under the name and style of L. G. Murphy & Co.
LAWce G. MURPHY.
EMIL FRITZ.
Fort Stanton, N. M., Nov 19th, 1869.   44-4t

This dissolution notice ran in the Santa Fe New Mexican on December 28, 1869. It is not clear if J.A. LaRue joined the firm at its inception before 1868 or at a later date. By all accounts, Murphy, Fritz, and LaRue continued doing business together in other ways after the dissolution and LaRue would later go into mining and cattle business with future firm member James J. Dolan.

The Santa Fe New Mexican
Tuesday, Dec 28, 1869

out of the Army later that year. By 1868, the new company had been issued a license to sell retail liquor and was operating a brewery and store near the eastern boundary of the Fort Stanton military reservation.[18] As home to the Mescalero Indian Agency, the two men quickly realized the economic potential that Fort Stanton and the region presented to those who controlled the supply of goods needed by the Army and the agency and began using their connections and war-time reputations to lay the foundations of something much more significant.[19]

The position of Post Trader at Fort Stanton represented a profitable opportunity for *L.G. Murphy and Company*. On April 28, 1868, the War Department officially awarded Murphy a license to serve as the post-sutler at Fort Stanton. However, later testimony by Murphy himself indicates the firm operated on the post as early as 1866.[20] *L.G. Murphy and Company* also received a license to trade with the Mescalero Apache. At the time, however, there were very few members of the tribe in the area around Fort Stanton following their departure from the Bosque Redondo reservation in November 1865. Murphy and Fritz relocated their firm's headquarters to a new eighteen-room trading post a few hundred yards from the fort's parade ground, expanding *L.G. Murphy and Company* into an economic powerhouse in Lincoln County. The building soon became a center of social life at the post and boasted a store, a billiard parlor, a dance hall, and an unlicensed saloon.[21] It was also sometime between 1866 and 1868 that Murphy and Fritz opened a branch store in *La Placita* (Lincoln). The firm located this smaller operation near the middle of *La Placita*, in an adobe building that Murphy would later sell to Alexander McSween for use as his home. Virginia native Alexander Duval operated the firm's store and ran a hotel with the business.[22] Despite increasing profits, the firm lost a partner in 1869. LaRue withdrew from the partnership in November of that year, leaving complete control of the firm in the hands of Murphy and Fritz.[23]

With the departure of LaRue, the firm looked toward new employees and potential partners to assist in growing the business into the next decade. Murphy hired fellow Irishmen and Army veterans John R. Bolton and James J. Dolan as head clerk and assistant clerk, respectively. Bolton was 36 years old, a former Army quartermaster, and by all accounts, an even-tempered and respected community member. James J. Dolan, on the other hand, was only 21 years old, ambitious, and hot-tempered—a perfect fit for the growing firm of *L.G. Murphy and Company*. Dolan had mustered out of the Army at

The Post Sutler Store at Fort Stanton, headquarters of *L.G. Murphy & Company*, c.1872
Lincoln County Historical Society

Fritz and Murphy's relationship with officers at Fort Stanton is on full display in this picture taken in front of the Commanding Officer's Quarters between 1871 and 1872.
(L to R) Post Surgeon Charles Steyer, Lt. Orsemus Boyd, Emil Fritz, Lt. Casper Conrad, Captain William McCleave, Lt. Colonel Augustus V. Kautz, Mrs. Mckibbin, Captain Chambers McKibbin, Mrs. Boyd, L.G. Murphy.
Lincoln County Historical Society

Fort Stanton in April 1869 as a musician and almost immediately began working for the company.[24]

With their primary business secured and growing, Murphy and Fritz turned their attention toward new personal and professional endeavors. With help from Murphy and others, former Army Captain and longtime Lincoln County resident Saturnino Baca won the election to the territorial legislature in 1868. With support from his constituents, Representative Baca introduced the bill authorizing the creation of Lincoln County. Following Territorial statutes, the new county held a special election to fill the Probate Judge and Sheriff positions. Once voters filled these positions, the men were authorized to appoint the remainder of county positions until they scheduled a regular election. There are records of an election being held in Lincoln sometime during the spring of 1869, but the event, according to the *Santa Fe Weekly Post*, "...resulted in a confusion of ideas which leaves a doubt as to which party gained."[25] It seems that the territorial government did not accept the results of this election. On May 12, Territorial Governor H.H. Heath appointed Murphy as Probate Judge and Mauricio Sanchez as County Sheriff.[26] The county held a regular election in the fall of 1869, selecting Murphy to serve in the critical position of Probate Judge—one he held off and on until 1876. Beyond politics, Murphy and Fritz also looked to expand their business interests. In 1870, the entrepreneurs financially backed a new placer mining operation in the Jicarilla mountains, north of Fort Stanton. With their help, workers dug an artesian well to power a sluice.[27] No further mention of the endeavor is recorded, with the assumption that the effort did not prove profitable.

By the late 1860s, the company and its members had aligned themselves with the powerful Santa Fe Ring—a network of corrupt politicians and businessmen within the territory—using their connections to expand their empire in Lincoln County. These men included U.S. District Attorney Stephen B. Elkins, New Mexico Attorney General Thomas B. Catron, and eventually Territorial Governor Samuel B. Axtell. Despite their favored status among high-ranking territorial officials, the company's standing with the U.S. Army lay solely in the hands of Secretary of War William W. Belknap. The coveted post-sutler and Indian Trader positions quickly became political tools. In October 1870, Murphy lost his status as Post Trader when the Army appointed Santa Fe auctioneer and politician Richard M. Stephens to the position.[28] Armed with letters of endorsement signed by every officer at Fort Stanton, Murphy and Fritz traveled to Washington D.C. and met personally with Secretary of War Belknap. Belknap refused to reinstate Murphy

L.G. Murphy & Company, c.1871-1872
(L to R) James Dolan, Emil Fritz, William Martin, L.G. Murphy
Lincoln County Historical Society

as the Post Trader but assured the men they could keep their property. With their property secured and a license to trade with the Apache, Murphy, Fritz, and Dolan imposed their will on anyone the Army sent to do business at Fort Stanton. Richard Stephens resigned soon after Murphy and Fritz returned from Washington, and the next three Post Traders either sold their licenses back to *L.G. Murphy and Company* or never opened the store's doors.[29] Through bribery and intimidation, *L.G. Murphy and Company* maintained their stranglehold over Fort Stanton—but their time in control was running out.

In 1870, President Ulysses S. Grant transferred control of the Indian Agencies in New Mexico from the U.S. Army to the Department of the Interior. That same year, newly appointed Mescalero Agent, Lieutenant Argulus G. Hennisee, succeeded in establishing an official Indian Agency for the Mescalero Apache at Fort Stanton. This fortunate turn of events created a new opportunity for *L.G. Murphy and Company* to profit from the Army and agency's needs. They would require a large amount of food and supplies to support a reservation filled with Mescalero Apache. The most significant obstacles standing between the firm and unchecked wealth were the men appointed by the Department of the Interior to oversee the agency and reservation. However, the company was not above intimidation, force, and unscrupulous business practices to counter resistance from the government. The new Mescalero Agent, Andrew Jackson Curtis, arrived at Fort Stanton in June 1871 and settled into his office inside the Post Trader building owned by *L.G. Murphy and Company*. There is no doubt that Curtis favored Murphy and Fritz' firm during his tenure at Fort Stanton—although the company's lack of competition certainly contributed to their relationship.

In barely a year, Curtis granted government contracts worth more than $57,000 to the company. He and Superintendent of Indian Affairs Nathaniel Pope agreed that awarding contracts without advertising for bids was the best way to meet their obligation to feed and clothe the Mescalero Apache men, women, and children living at the reser-

Mescalero Apache at Fort Stanton, c.1872-1878
Lincoln County Historical Society

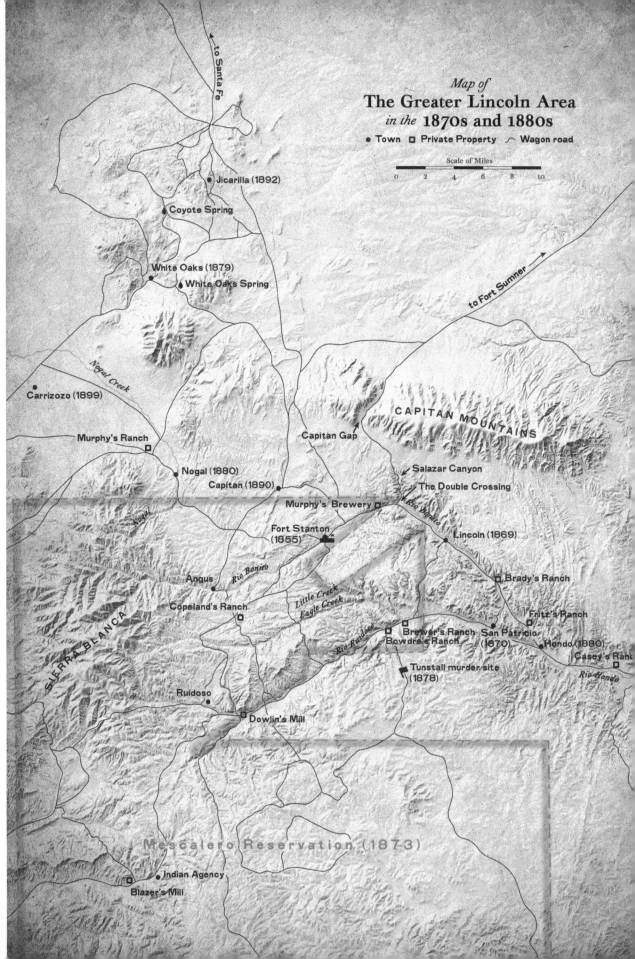

Map of
The Greater Lincoln Area
in the **1870s and 1880s**

● Town   ▢ Private Property   ⌒ Wagon road

Scale of Miles

0   2   4   6   8   10

to Santa Fe

to Fort Sumner

● Jicarilla (1892)

● Coyote Spring

● White Oaks (1879)
● White Oaks Spring

Nogal Creek

● Carrizozo (1899)

▢ Murphy's Ranch

CAPITAN MOUNTAINS

Capitan Gap

← Salazar Canyon
The Double Crossing

● Nogal (1880)
Capitan (1890) ●

Murphy's Brewery ▢

Rio Bonito

● Lincoln (1869)

Fort Stanton
(1855) ▣

Nogal

Angus ●

Rio Bonito

▢ Brady's Ranch

Copeland's Ranch ●

Little Creek
Eagle Creek

▢ Fritz's Ranch

SIERRA BLANCA

Rio Ruidoso

▢ Brewer's Ranch   San Patricio
Bowdre's Ranch   (1870)

Hondo (1880) ●

Casey's Ranch ▢

■ Tunstall murder site
(1878)

Rio Hondo

● Ruidoso

▢ Dowlin's Mill

Mescalero Reservation (1873)

● Indian Agency
▢ Blazer's Mill

vation. Although, serious questions began to arise regarding the number of Mescalero Apache residing on the reservations and whether Curtis was overestimating numbers due to pressure from *L.G. Murphy and Company*. By inflating the number of Apache on the reservation, Murphy and Fritz walked away with a surplus of goods already paid for by the federal government. The firm then resold the excess supplies to local ranchers, farmers, and fellow merchants. This ruse was the firm's most effective scheme to inflate its profit margin, and Curtis seemed inclined to assist them in their endeavor. In the fall of 1871, Curtis claimed that three-hundred and twenty-five Mescalero resided at the reservation—by 1872, the number he reported skyrocketed to nearly three thousand.[30]

Commissioner of Indian Affairs Francis H. Walker disagreed with Curtis and Pope's recommendations to forgo competitive bidding for the reservation. In the fall of 1872, the Army solicited bids for supplying the Mescalero Agency with corn, beef, and other goods. The Army awarded the beef contract to Pecos Valley broker Van C. Smith. Smith's cattle supplier was a newcomer to Lincoln County, John Henry Riley. Riley, another native of Ireland, came to New Mexico through Colorado, where he worked as a clerk for the Colorado Central Railroad. Riley moved south to New Mexico, starting a ranch and serving as a clerk for another of L.G. Murphy and Company's competitors, beef contractor Rockwell Blake.[31] Unfortunately for Smith and Riley, Curtis had already signed an agreement with Dolan without consent from his superiors. This act cost the U.S. Government nearly $3,000 and cast serious doubts about Curtis' impartiality.[32] Curtis resigned, claiming ill health and low pay as his reasoning, and in January 1873, the Secretary of the Interior appointed a new Agent for the Mescalero tribe—Samuel Bushnell.[33] Unfortunately for *L.G. Murphy and Company*, this new agent was neither incompetent nor willing to look the other way, and suddenly their sovereignty faced its greatest challenge yet.

Accompanied by his adult son Charles, Samuel Bushnell arrived at Fort Stanton in April of 1873 and immediately began investigating the actions of his predecessor. Bushnell quickly realized that *L.G. Murphy and Company* controlled every aspect of trade with the Mescalero Apache and the U.S. Army. Bushnell was not alone in his assessment, learning disturbing details about the depth of corruption at Fort Stanton from those not silenced by Murphy's influence. Those willing to talk to and work with Bushnell included Captain James Randlett of the Eighth Cavalry, who arrived at Fort Stanton in April 1872.[34] Soon after his arrival, Randlett began reporting to his superiors on the state of affairs at

Fort Stanton, including complaints that L.G. Murphy and Company were taking advantage of enlisted men by selling goods at outrageous prices. According to Randlett, when he confronted the firm about their prices, he "was met with insults."[35] Randlett's outspoken criticism of Murphy and Fritz increased over time and, by the summer of 1873, placed him squarely at odds with the firm

To expose *L.G. Murphy and Company's* corrupt nature, Bushnell secured a job for his son within the firm so that he might learn the "inner and secret workings" of Murphy's net-

James F. Randlett during his Civil War service as a Lt. Colonel in the New Hampshire Volunteers
Lincoln County Historical Society

work.[36] This plan appears to have paid off as Bushnell soon claimed in official letters to have found strong evidence demonstrating a complicated web of corruption. Bushnell started his long list of accusations by accurately accounting exactly how many Mescalero Apache resided at Fort Stanton. Bushnell contradicted Curtis' claims, stating that only two-hundred Apache visited the agency during his first month at Fort Stanton. Bushnell requested Superintendent of Indian Affairs L. Edwin Dudley find a replacement for L.G. Murphy, informing his superior that Murphy had told him it did not, "make any difference who the government sends here as agent. We control these Indians. I'll turn the Apaches loose on the military. I can do it any day."[37] Despite this warning and threats against Bushnell and his staff, the Department of the Interior declined to remove Murphy from the post. Despite this initial setback, Samuel Bushnell seemed determined to bring order to the chaotic situation—starting with removing *L.G. Murphy and Company* from the equation.

Beyond their mounting troubles with the government officials at Fort Stanton, L.G. Murphy's original partner, Emil Fritz's health was failing, and he was planning an extended trip back to his native Germany.[38] Fritz began to make final plans in case of his death, and in May 1873, he traveled to Santa Fe to visit doctors and ascertain his chances of recovery. Perhaps knowing that Fritz would possibly never return to New Mexico, Murphy reorganized his company in June of 1873, admitting James Dolan as a junior partner and hiring John Henry Riley as a clerk.

In Fritz's absence, the hotheaded Dolan and increasingly drunk Murphy allowed tensions at Fort Stanton to turn violent and escalate to the point of no return. Bushnell concluded that moving the headquarters for the Mescalero Agency altogether could effectively remove. Murphy's control over the situation. In May 1873, Bushnell visited several surrounding ranches and villages in search of a new headquarters for the Mescalero Agency, enlisting Captain Randlett's and John Riley's assistance. It is unclear exactly why John Riley assisted Bushnell and Randlett's efforts to locate a new headquarters—as relocating the agency would undoubtedly harm the operations of *L.G. Murphy and Company*. According to Captain Randlett, Riley confided in him at the time of their reconnaissance trip that he was "at outs with Murphy and Co."[39] Riley's actions angered his colleague, James Dolan, and on Sunday, May 8th, 1873, the two men's anger boiled over. That evening, Captain Randlett discovered Dolan and Riley "quarreling" in his post quarters. Randlett intervened and invited Riley to board until the men could settle the matter. Riley and Randlett attended church service that evening, during which Riley admitted that he feared that Dolan intended to shoot and kill him.

After the church service, Dolan tracked down Riley and Randlett and began an increasingly heated argument. Murphy quickly inserted himself into the fray, and witnesses later stated that Dolan and Murphy appeared drunk during the altercation. As Randlett stepped in and attempted to diffuse the situation, Dolan drew his *Smith and Wesson* pistol and leveled it at Riley's head. Fearing for his friend's life, Captain Randlett attempted to disarm Dolan just as the gun discharged, narrowly missing its mark. Randlett immediately ordered the arrest of Dolan and Murphy, charging the younger man with assault with intent to kill. Randlett released Murphy later on the night of the incident. Still, Dolan remained in custody until morning when Murphy filed a *writ of habeas corpus* with Captain Chambers McKibbin, commanding officer at the post.[40] Although released from custody, Captain McKibbin acquiesced to Captain Randlett's request that James Dolan be escorted from the post and not permitted to return. Dolan did not remain absent from Stanton for long, however. Upon his return from Santa Fe, an ailing Emil Fritz petitioned Captain McKibbin to allow Dolan back on post to assist him with arranging his personal

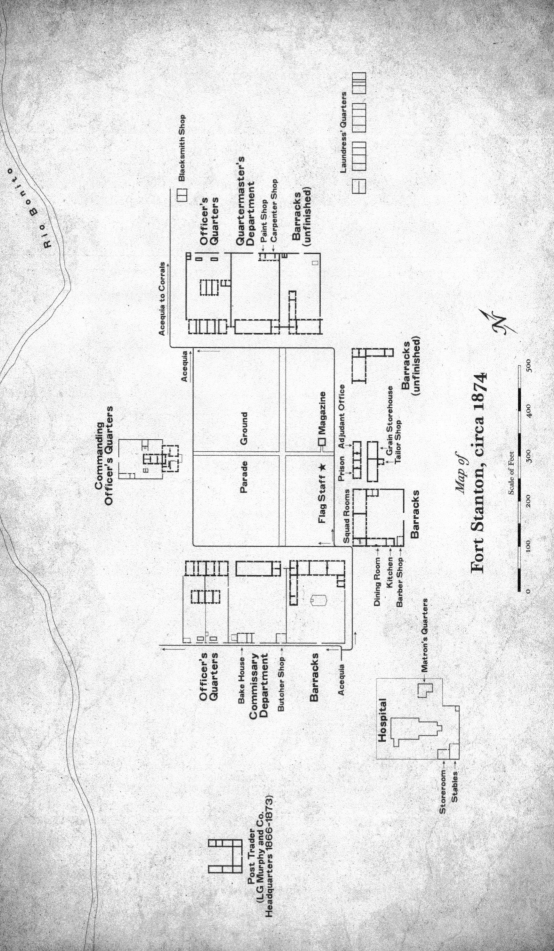

Rio Bonito

Blacksmith Shop

Officer's Quarters

Quartermaster's Department

Paint Shop
Carpenter Shop

Barracks (unfinished)

Acequia to Corrals

Acequia

Laundress' Quarters

Commanding Officer's Quarters

Parade Ground

Acequia

Barracks (unfinished)

Grain Storehouse

Tailor Shop

Flag Staff ★

Magazine

Prison

Adjudant Office

Squad Rooms

Barracks

Dining Room
Kitchen
Barber Shop

Officer's Quarters

Bake House

Commissary Department

Butcher Shop

Barracks

Acequia

Hospital

Matron's Quarters

Storeroom
Stables

Post Trader (LG Murphy and Co. Headquarters 1866-1873)

N

Map of
Fort Stanton, circa 1874

Scale of Feet

0   100   200   300   400   500

and business affairs. McKibbin conferred with Randlett on the matter, and both men agreed.[41]

Although this incident occurred on federal property and involved an Army officer, the War Department turned the case over to civilian authorities as it involved a private citizen. At his initial hearing before Probate Judge Saturnino Baca, Dolan argued that his pistol had discharged accidentally and that Randlett's story had changed multiple times. Murphy also testified on Dolan's behalf, and the judge elected not to indict the young Irishman on any counts. On the contrary, Captain Randlett found himself in serious legal trouble related to his confrontation with Dolan. In retaliation, Dolan formally accused Captain Randlett of assault and a grand jury indicted the officer during the July 1873

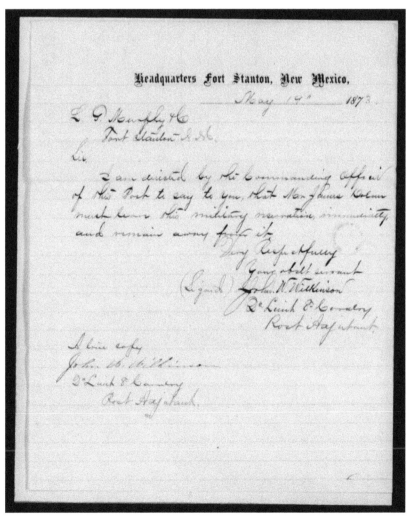

Copy of letter, dated May 19, 1873, ordering James Dolan removed from Fort Stanton by order of Commanding Officer Chambers McKibbin
National Archives and Records Administration

term of the district court held in Lincoln. District Judge Warren Bristol then issued a warrant for Randlett's apprehension, and County Sheriff Jacob "Jack" Gylam arrested and charged the Army Captain in July 1873.[42] At the court's fall term, Randlett successfully beat the assault charge, but Murphy and his allies continued to attack the officer through the courts. On December 20, 1873, the Horrell Brothers and their allies attacked a wedding party in Lincoln, killing four men and wounding several others. They conducted this attack in retaliation for the killing of their brother by a citizen posse from Lincoln on December 1, 1873, continuing their campaign of terror by indiscriminately attacking Hispanic citizens as they fled Lincoln County for Texas. In the aftermath of these attacks, a grand jury indicted twenty-six men for their alleged roles in the affair, including two of Murphy's enemies, Captain James Randlett and rancher Robert Casey. Accused of murder, Randlett's attorney requested and received a change of venue to Socorro County. The jury in the case took very little time to deliberate, ultimately exonerating Randlett completely. Captain Randlett beat the charges, but learned a valuable lesson regarding the reach of *L.G. Murphy and Company* and the consequences of challenging the Santa Fe Ring.

While leadership at the Department of the Interior considered moving the Mescalero Agency Headquarters, Agent Bushnell and Superintendent Dudley focused on Murphy's physical property at Fort Stanton. Because Murphy owned the Post Sutler Store, he and his firm controlled all storage and issuance of goods to the Mescalero Apache.[43] Bushnell and Dudley recommended that the Department of the Interior construct new buildings to house the agency headquarters and distance themselves from *L.G. Murphy and Company*. After securing estimates for the new construction, Superintendent Dudley concluded that purchasing the existing store from Murphy was the best course of action.[44] Murphy offered to sell the building for $10,000.00, and after negotiations, the Department of the Interior agreed to purchase the structure for $8,000.00. The parties finalized the sale on June 13, 1873. However, the Department of the Interior would only pay Murphy once the deed arrived at their office in Washington, D.C., and Murphy refused to send the document until the War Department paid him in full.[45] A stalemate ensued, during which *L.G. Murphy and Company* continued to occupy and operate from the building. Without assistance from the Army, Bushnell was powerless to remove L.G. Murphy from the Post Sutler store, and Murphy maintained a friendly relationship with the post's commander, Chambers Mckibbin.

The Randlett incident and increasingly clear evidence of corruption uncovered by Samuel Bushnell and L. Edwin Dudley provided all three men enough leverage to request the War Department again remove *L.G. Murphy and Company* from Fort Stanton. On September 2, 1873, Superintendent Dudley arrived at Fort Stanton and demanded Murphy vacate the property within twenty-four hours. Murphy complied, and Agent Bushnell took immediate ownership of the building and control of the daily issuance of rations.[46] Despite their ouster from the sutler store, Murphy and Dolan remained at the post until September 30, 1873. On that day, Captain McKibbin, Commanding Officer of Fort Stanton, delivered Secretary of War Belknap's order that the men were to leave the post and escorted them from the fort. By all accounts, the men left Fort Stanton with some dignity intact and perhaps with one final deadly parting shot.

Secretary of War William C. Belknap, a protege of William Sherman, controlled the issuing of Indian Trader and Post Sutler licenses after 1870. In 1876, the U.S. Senate accused Belknap of corruption related to issuance of licenses and kickbacks he received from several sutlers. He resigned in March 1876 but the Senate elected to hold hearings anyway. The committee acquitted Belknap but his political career was ruined.
National Archives and Records Administration

On Monday, October 13th, 1873—just two weeks after the Army banned *L.G. Murphy and Company* from Fort Stanton—Charles Bushnell was found dead in his room at the former sutler's store. The only newspaper article regarding his death stated that he died from a self-administered morphine overdose. Although there is no direct evidence that Murphy or his associates had anything to do with the younger Bushnell's death, the timing is highly suspicious. Bushnell might have been one of the first victims of Murphy and Dolan's quest to increase their power—a list that would eventually include Robert Casey, John Tunstall, Alexander McSween, and at least a dozen other men.

CHAPTER THREE
BUILDING THE HOUSE

L.G. Murphy's influence at Fort Stanton remained strong despite his physical removal. Shortly after *L.G. Murphy and Company's* departure, the War Department appointed Paul Dowlin as post trader.[1] Dowlin, a native of Pennsylvania, enlisted in the 1st New Mexico Volunteers in September 1861, eventually gaining a commission in 1862 and mustering out of service as a captain in May 1866.[2] Dowlin served with L.G. Murphy and Emil Fritz during the war and settled along the Rio Ruidoso with his brother after his military service ended. Dowlin was an ally of Murphy and contracted with his friend for the goods he sold at the Post Sutler Store.

Further diluting the Army's actions against Murphy, James Dolan secured a license to trade with the Mescalero Apache. The firm cut a deal with John Riley and William Rynerson to provide them with affordable beef to fulfill their remaining government contracts.[3] Undeterred by their eviction from Fort Stanton, Murphy, Dolan, and Riley viewed their predicament as only a minor setback, setting their sights on a new location for their headquarters—the nearby town of Lincoln.

Since the establishment of Lincoln County in 1869, its namesake county seat continued to grow, eventually emerging as the economic and social center for the county. It seemed only fitting that the most influential business in the region constructs its headquarters in the largest and most important town. As it stood, the firm had already expanded into Lincoln, establishing a satellite store near the middle of the growing village in the early 1870s. By June 1873, *L.G. Murphy and Company* was advertising their Lincoln store in the *Santa Fe New Mexican*. The advertisements indicated that the firm was dealing in "groceries, liquors, and mining implements" and paying the "highest price for country produce, cattle, etc."[4] Despite their established presence, clear ownership of the property did not exist for the land on which the current store sat, nor where they planned to construct their new building. Though he began construction on his new store in 1873, Murphy did not officially file on the eighty-acre tract with the Land Office in Mesilla until 1877. He did not receive the patent—issued and signed by President Rutherford B. Hayes—until June 1878. The simple reason is that until 1875, no official survey of lands in the Bonito Valley existed, and no land office existed with which to file a claim.

The Territorial Land Office in Mesilla did not open until 1875. Almost immediately after it did, Lawyer—and former District Attorney—John D. Bail filed on property in Lincoln. Bail was a known ally of the Santa Fe Ring, so his choice to file on property already improved on by his presumptive friend, L.G. Murphy, could indicate a growing rift between Murphy, Fritz, and at least certain members of the Santa Fe Ring. In the words of his lawyer, John Newcomb, Murphy's improvements on the property included "a large and commodious dwelling house and store, said building and improvements costing your petitioner (Murphy) over twenty-thousand dollars."[5] Murphy wrote to the General Land Office in the fall of 1876, claiming he had attempted to file on the property but failed to do so because of "willful negligence" by this lawyer. The letter also claimed that Bail had only filed on the property "for the purpose of being avenged upon said affiant, and for no other purpose." Murphy initially filed a formal protest over Bail's application for the patent but withdrew the complaint through a letter drafted by John Newcomb to the Commissioner of the General Land Office, dated December 2, 1876. In the letter, which both L.G. Murphy and John Bail signed, Newcomb asserted that the,

> *Differences between said grantees, having this day been amicably settled and*
> *arranged that said protest and petition of said Murphy be and the same*
> *is hereby withdrawn and that the patent for the land in question shall*
> *pass to the said John Bail and that the same when issued shall be forwarded to*
> *the said Lawrence G. Murphy of Lincoln, Lincoln County New Mexico, who is*
> *hereby authorized to receive and receipt for the same.*[6]

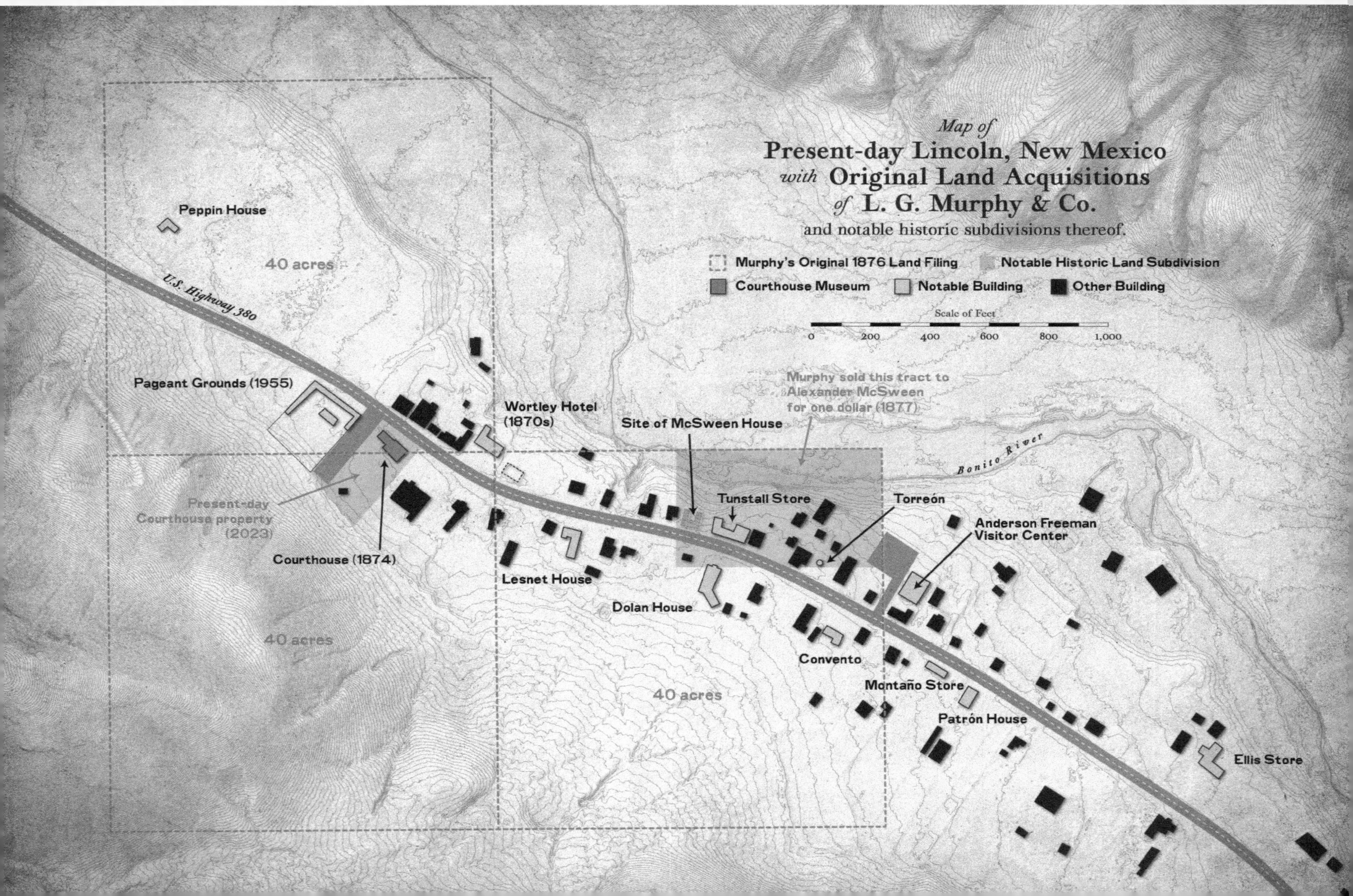

Map of
Present-day Lincoln, New Mexico
with Original Land Acquisitions
of L. G. Murphy & Co.
and notable historic subdivisions thereof.

Murphy's Original 1876 Land Filing   Notable Historic Land Subdivision
Notable Building   Other Building
Courthouse Museum

Scale of Feet

0   200   400   600   800   1,000

Bonito River

Ellis Store

Patrón House

Montaño Store

Convento

Anderson Freeman
Visitor Center

Torreón

Murphy sold this tract to
Alexander McSween
for one dollar (1877)

Tunstall Store

Dolan House

Site of McSween House

40 acres

Lesnet House

Wortley Hotel
(1870s)

Peppin House

40 acres

U.S. Highway 380

Pageant Grounds (1955)

Courthouse (1874)

Present-day
Courthouse property
(2023)

40 acres

The cause of the animosity between the two men is unclear, but they settled the matter when Murphy purchased the property from Bail in 1876. Murphy refiled on the property with the Mesilla Land Office in February 1877. The patent, signed by President Rutherford B. Hayes, was issued on June 24th, 1878, only 118 days before Murphy's death and after he had left Lincoln for the last time.

The company hired builder George Peppin to oversee the construction of their new store and headquarters. A native of Vermont, George Warden Peppin immigrated to the California goldfields in the 1850s, working primarily as a builder. In October 1861, he enlisted in Company "A" of the 1st California Volunteer Infantry Regiment, joining the "California Column" on its 900-mile march across Arizona and New Mexico. Once in New Mexico, Peppin spent the war moving between forts throughout the territory. After mustering out of the Army, he moved to Fort Stanton, where the Army hired him as a civilian builder and mason. Peppin's experience building and repairing structures for the military undoubtedly influenced the design of the new headquarters for *L.G. Murphy and Company*. In particular, the building's two-story design, territorial style windows and doors, and hipped roof were more common on the East Coast than in the Southwest.

It is unclear exactly when construction began on the impressive structure, but workers had completed a substantial portion of the building by the early winter of 1873. The company also noted in their business ledger on November 5th, 1873, that they had paid a man named L. Dickens for eighty-one days of labor on the structure up to November 1st.[7] This notation would set the construction date back to August 12th, 1873, at the earliest. Who L. Dickens was and what his role in the building's construction is not entirely clear. There is a Louis Dickens who listed himself in the 1860 territorial census as living in Santa Fe, working as a surveyor.[8] The

Builder, Master Mason, and Lincoln County Sheriff, George W. Peppin
Lincoln County Historical Society

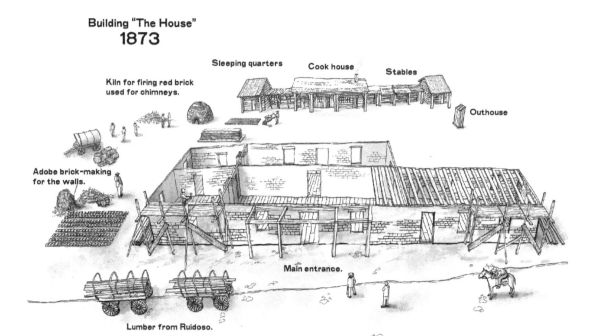

Building "The House"
1873

Sleeping quarters Cook house Stables

Kiln for firing red brick
used for chimneys.

Outhouse

Adobe brick-making
for the walls.

Main entrance.

Lumber from Ruidoso.

following year, he joined the New Mexico volunteers and granted a commission as a 1st Lieutenant. In 1862, before mustering out of the Army, Lieutenant Louis Dickens spent time at Fort Craig alongside future Lincoln County Sheriff William Brady and leading citizen Saturnino Baca.[9] It is highly likely that the L. Dickens employed by *L.G. Murphy and Company*, and the one that served in Company E of the 1st Regiment, New Mexico Infantry, are indeed the same person. Based on his previous work as a surveyor, it is likely that Murphy hired Dickens to lay out the building site for the laborers. Dickens completed his work by the fall of 1873 when full-scale construction commenced. By the end of the year, laborers had completed substantial work on the building, supported by a traumatic memory shared many years later by Lily Casey-Klasner. Klasner related that on December 20, 1873, terrified townspeople sought refuge in the partially completed structure following the deadly attack on the town by the Horrell brothers and their allies.[10]

Before beginning construction on the main building, Peppin supervised the construction of several outbuildings—including a brick kiln, carpenter's shop, and detached cookhouse. Sam Wortley fed the laborers from the mess hall, and the structure soon became known as Wortley's Mess. Local masons, including twenty-year-old Francisco Gomez, molded and dried adobe bricks on-site, and German immigrant Godfrey Gauss fired bricks to construct chimneys. Murphy purchased the lumber from a fellow Army

Veteran and newly appointed post trader at Fort Stanton, Captain Paul Dowlin. Dowlin's mill sat along the Rio Ruidoso and provided the lumber for many of the area's construction projects. According to records, Murphy purchased fifty-eight thousand board feet of lumber for the project, totaling $1,595.00.[11]

The building required thousands of handmade adobe bricks, which were large even by contemporary standards. The bricks measured eighteen inches long, nine inches wide, and four and one-half inches tall. Once dried, each brick weighed an astounding twenty pounds. Masons laid the bricks three courses deep on the first floor, making the walls an impressive twenty-seven inches thick. Once builders reached the second-floor joists, they added three-inch by twelve-inch wall plates made of white pine into the beams to support the next course of bricks. Above the first floor, the walls shrunk to a thickness of only eighteen inches, continuing to a total height of twenty feet from the foundation. The only exception to this reduction in thickness was in the western extension, where twenty-seven-inch walls extended to the second-floor ceiling. Workers might have added this extension after they completed the main section. The west wall dividing the main room and this section is the same thickness as all other exterior walls. In addition, the roof line of the western extension does not match that of the main building, and the floor heights are slightly different. Perhaps the construction of the building progressed at such a pace and within the budget that Murphy decided to expand the structure and include space for activities not essential to the business.

On November 5, 1873, Murphy ordered 58,000 board feet of lumber from Paul Dowlin and hired carpenter, R.H. Ewan. Almost all the lumber purchased from the mill was Southwestern White Pine (Pinus strobiformis), hauled thirty miles to Lincoln via oxcart. Ewan custom-crafted all the window sashes, mullions, molding, and trim on site,

Paul Dowlin's Mill along the Rio Ruidoso
Carmen Phillips Collection
Lincoln County Historical Society

53

joining everything with square nails. The lintels for the doors and windows were four inches wide by twelve inches high, and the original floor planks measured six inches wide by 5/4" thick. The account ledger for *L.G. Murphy and Company* reveals that by the end of 1873, the firm had spent at least $8,000.00 on materials and labor for the building, including $84.00 for the 4,200 shake shingles needed to cover the extensive roof line.

The first floor consisted of the retail store directly through the main front doors and faced north onto the street. The first floor also had a billiard room in the western extension, L.G. Murphy's office, and a warehouse room for storing the assortment of goods sold in the retail store. The northeast corner room on the first floor also served as Lincoln's post office, perhaps as early as 1874 when Irish immigrant and Army veteran John Bolton held the position of Post Master. In 1876 the Postmaster General appointed James Dolan to the post. Dolan's position as Post Master and the post office's location inside his company's headquarters, provided the firm a significant advantage in collecting intelligence regarding regional happenings. Murphy and his partners reserved the billiard room on the west end of the building to entertain friends and allies. Although the billiard room was attached to the store, local tradition indicates it had no interior access to the rest of the building. Patrons had to enter through the front and back doors while the proprietors passed drinks through a small window leading to the main store area.

The firm designed the east end of the second floor as a private living space. Murphy and Fritz would each have two-room apartments, with a bedroom and a sitting room. Across the hallway sat two additional single-room apartments, one reserved for junior partner James Dolan and one for Murphy's domestic servant, Elizabeth Lloyd. Carpets covered the floors throughout the entire second floor. Builders lowered the vaulted ceilings above the living quarters by stretching muslin cloth between the walls and then painting on a thin coat of lime plaster. This process caused the fabric to tighten and gave the appearance of a solid plaster ceiling.

Murphy was a prominent member of the Masonic fraternity, belonging to Montezuma Lodge No.1, located in Santa Fe.[12] Above the billiard hall was a room Murphy hoped to use as a Masonic Lodge. Murphy petitioned the Grand Lodge of New Mexico to grant him a charter for a lodge in Lincoln. In this petition, he noted that the room was secure and only accessible by a ladder attached to the south-facing wall. The Grand Lodge of New Mexico did not grant Murphy a charter for a local Masonic Lodge, and it is unclear if he ever held any clandestine fraternal meetings in the room.

In addition to the mess hall and carpenter's shop, the rear of the property included stables, storage sheds, and a granary. The builders enclosed all of these outbuildings with an adobe wall, adding gates near the south corners of the building to allow teamsters to drive their wagons directly to the rear of the building. With the completion of the outbuildings and security wall, building stood ready for occupation—looming over the quiet town of Lincoln as by far the most prominent and grandest building in Lincoln.

L. G. Murphy and Company held a grand opening for their new store on June 4, 1874. Twenty-two days later, Emil Fritz died in Germany, never seeing the new store or inhabiting the living quarters built for him. In August 1874, just two months after his partner's death, Murphy reorganized his namesake business and promoted James Dolan to senior partner. It is unclear whether Dolan or someone else inhabited the room intended for Fritz following his death, though the company may have used the space for storage. Shortly after opening, local citizens began referring to the new building, as, "The House," a nickname used to reference both the building and *L. G. Murphy and Company.*

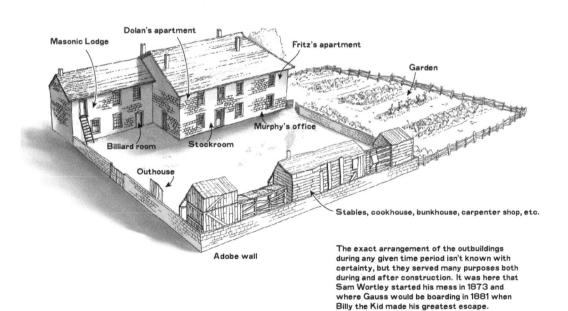

Rear View Of L. G. Murphy & Co.
1874

Masonic Lodge

Dolan's apartment

Fritz's apartment

Garden

Murphy's office

Billiard room

Stockroom

Outhouse

Stables, cookhouse, bunkhouse, carpenter shop, etc.

Adobe wall

The exact arrangement of the outbuildings during any given time period isn't known with certainty, but they served many purposes both during and after construction. It was here that Sam Wortley started his mess in 1873 and where Gauss would be boarding in 1881 when Billy the Kid made his greatest escape.

L.G. Murphy & Co., Lower Level
1874

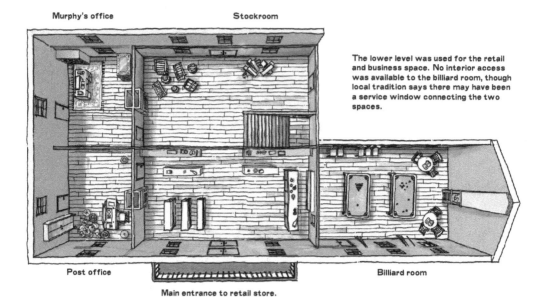

Murphy's office

Stockroom

The lower level was used for the retail and business space. No interior access was available to the billiard room, though local tradition says there may have been a service window connecting the two spaces.

Post office

Billiard room

Main entrance to retail store.

L.G. Murphy & Co., Upper Level
1874

The upper level was the living quarters, was well-appointed with furnishings, and reportedly was carpeted. No interior access was available to the Masonic Lodge, and access could only be gained via ladder to an exterior door.

Emil Fritz's bedroom used for storage.

Fritz's sitting room used as bunk room.

Hallway

Dolan's apartment.

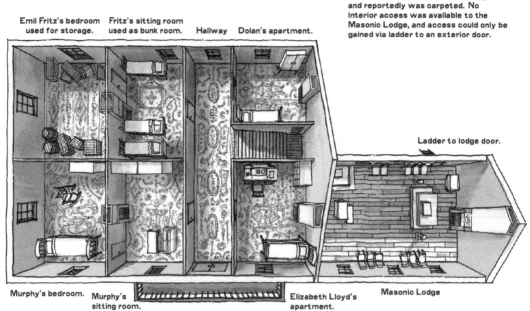

Ladder to lodge door.

Murphy's bedroom.

Murphy's sitting room.

Elizabeth Lloyd's apartment.

Masonic Lodge

CHAPTER FOUR
THE FALL OF THE HOUSE OF MURPHY

When the new building opened in 1874, it rapidly became the most well-stocked mercantile in the region. In November of 1874, *L.G. Murphy and Company* ordered thirteen tons of goods from *Seligman Brothers and Company* and *Staab and Company* in Santa Fe—stocking their new store with everything from liquor and guns to nails and clothing. This imposing edifice quickly became known locally as "The House," a name extended to the company's members and network of corrupt officials and hired thugs. Within a year of being cast out of Fort Stanton, *L.G. Murphy, and Company* had reestablished itself and commanded its growing empire from the halls of the region's most impressive building. Despite their apparent position of power, *L.G. Murphy and Company* was losing money and already moving down a slow and steady path toward financial ruin.

One of the first deaths associated with the building occurred just four months after it opened. Late in the evening of October 21st, 1874, Lincoln County Deputy Sheriff Lyon Phillipowski entered the *L.G. Murphy, and Company* store. According to newspaper accounts, an extremely intoxicated Phillipowski began insulting and threatening William Burns, a clerk working for *L.G. Murphy and Company*. It is unclear why Phillipowski assaulted Burns, but the argument escalated to the point that Phillipowski called Burns out into the street. Burns armed himself and stepped outside, at which point Phillipowski began firing at him. Burns returned fire and mortally wounded the Deputy. A coroner's inquest held the following day determined that Burns had acted in self-defense and ordered him released from custody.[1] Speculation over the true motive for the killing

Lyon Phillipowski was born in Poland in 1836 and immigrated to California in 1859. He joined the Army in 1861 and traveled with the California Column to New Mexico. He served as Probate Clerk in Lincoln County before becoming a Deputy Sheriff shortly before his death in 1874. He left a widow and a young daughter behind after his death.

surfaced almost immediately, with rumors spreading that Murphy and Dolan orchestrated the murder because of the deputy's opposition to their organization and rising star as a member of the political community.

The violent death of Deputy Phillpowski was not the only fatal event to occur during the years the building served the community as a store. On September 2, 1876, future Regulator Josiah "Doc" Scurlock accidentally killed his friend Mike G. Harkins in the carpenter shop behind the *L.G. Murphy, and Company s*tore. Scurlock, who was on friendly terms with Murphy and Dolan then, showed his friend a new double-action pistol when it accidentally discharged, sending a bullet directly through Harkins' heart.[2] Just months before the Lincoln County War's most violent period erupted, Dolan shot and killed Hiraldo Jaramillo, claiming self-defense. According to Dolan, the young man grabbed hold of him while they were in the corral behind the store and began slashing at him with a knife. Dolan pulled his pocket pistol and shot the man in the hand and arm, but he continued to attack him. Finally, Dolan fired a final shot through Jaramillo's heart, killing him instantly. Dolan turned himself over to authorities, who released him after determining he acted in self-defense.[3] Locals found it very suspicious that Jaramillo's widow quickly remarried Dolan's close friend and ally, George Peppin.

John Riley, c.1880
Lincoln County Historical Society

By 1876 *L.G. Murphy and Company* was falling deeper and deeper into debt. In October 1876, Murphy and Dolan sold a minority interest in the firm to cattle broker and rancher John Riley. Riley brought lucrative U.S. Army cattle and grain contracts to the firm, but the company's fortunes were only about to worsen. In 1875, 32-year-old lawyer Alexander McSween moved to Lincoln with his wife, Susan. The young lawyer specialized in debt collection and immediately took on *L.G. Murphy and Company* as a client.

Despite McSween's success in collecting many of the debts owed to the firm, *L.G. Murphy and Company's* accounts remained in the red.[4] In January 1877, Probate Judge Florencio Gonzales oversaw examining the account books from the former partnership of L.G. Murphy and Emil Fritz. The analysis revealed that various parties owed the firm $25,000. Murphy needed to collect this money quickly so he turned to McSween for help. With little or no cash to pay the lawyer, Murphy likely compensated McSween by selling him a six-acre parcel of land along the north side of the road in Lincoln for the sum of $1.00. The property included the original *L.G. Murphy and Company* store building, which McSween renovated and expanded into his private home, as well as the property where McSween and Englishman John Tunstall would soon build their rival store.[5] Murphy fell ill about this time and, in March 1877, retired from the business, passing the reins to Dolan and Riley. The firm reorganized as *J.J. Dolan and Company* on March 14th, 1877, taking ownership of the large store in Lincoln and assuming all of the company's debts.[6]

Although the solvency of *J.J. Dolan and Company* looked bleak on paper, by all outward appearances, the firm was still very much a lucrative and profitable endeavor. The company's alliances with leaders in the Santa Fe Ring remained strong. On April 28th, 1876, Territorial Governor Samuel B. Axtell visited Lincoln for the first time as a guest of

L.G. Murphy. Axtell's trip marked the first time on record that a Governor of New Mexico visited Lincoln, and Axtell lodged with Murphy in the spare quarters on the second floor of "The House."[7] In a twist of historical irony, Axtell's high-profile visit to Lincoln occurred precisely five years to the day before Billy the Kid's escape from the same building in 1881.

As the most violent period of the Lincoln County War lingered on the horizon, Dolan and Riley's financial troubles continued to grow. By the time the conflict ignited in February 1878, the men's financial futures were in ruins. Throughout 1877, the firm's relationship with McSween deteriorated rapidly after a dispute erupted over the lawyer's attempts to collect Emil Fritz's $10,000.00 life insurance policy, listing the company as the beneficiary. The feud escalated after McSween expanded his business interests with his new partners—cattle baron John Chisum and Englishman John Henry Tunstall. Mounting debt and the new competition in Lincoln finally pushed *J.J. Dolan and Company* to the breaking point. In January 1878, the firm drafted an agreement with Thomas B. Catron to mortgage their large store building, 40 surrounding acres, all remaining goods, and 1,500 head of cattle. In return, Catron acted as a guarantor for money owed by the firm to the First National Bank of Santa Fe, and *J.S. Johnson and Company*. Catron also offered to loan the men up to $25,000.00.[8]

Fueled by resentment over his financial situation, Dolan and his allies increased their attacks upon McSween, Tunstall, and Chisum. In early February 1878, McSween and Tunstall appeared in court at Mesilla to defend accusations that McSween had mishandled the money received from Emil Fritz's life insurance policy. Judge Warren Bristol set a trial date for the April term of court in Lincoln but issued a writ of attachment for McSween's property. Under the guise of serving this writ against the property of McSween's business partner John Tunstall, Dolan orchestrated the cold-blooded murder of the young Englishman, kicking off the exceptionally violent events collectively

Thomas B. Catron, c.1885
Lincoln County Historical Society

known as the Lincoln County War. During the next several months, "The House" served periodically as a barracks, mess hall, and hospital for forces loyal to Dolan and Riley.

On February 20th, 1878, members of the posse that had gunned down John Tunstall gathered at the "The House," most likely to celebrate their victory. Sheriff William Brady, an ally of Murphy, Dolan, and Riley, frequently used the building as his unofficial office, and was actively shielding those responsible for Tunstall's murder from justice. That morning, two duly deputized Special Constables, William H. Bonney and Fred Waite, along with elected Constable Atanacio Martinez, attempted to serve legal warrants for the arrest of numerous men accused of having a hand in Tunstall's brutal slaying. Unfortunately for them, the power of "The House" was on full display that day, and when the lawmen entered the building, Sheriff Brady turned the tables on them. Brady refused to allow the arrest of those accused of Tunstall's murder and used his superior numbers to arrest the Constables for unstated crimes.

In April 1878, Dolan and Riley posted an advertisement in the *Santa Fe New Mexican*, blaming the outbreak of violence in Lincoln County for disrupting their business so significantly that they needed to close their store. They assured the public they would reopen after conditions improved—a promise they would not be able to keep. Following Dolan and Riley's closure, Thomas Catron sent his brother-in-law, Edgar Walz, to Lincoln. Walz aimed to secure his family's new investment and take over operations at the former *J.J. Dolan and Company* store.

On April 29, 1878, members of the *Seven Rivers Warriors* and *Jesse Evans Gang* ambushed three allies of McSween near the ranch of Charles Fritz. These two gangs were well known in the area and had worked with and for L.G. Murphy and James Dolan in the past, rustling cattle to fulfill the men's government contracts. The Murphy partisans killed Frank McNab, seriously wounded Ab Saunders, and captured Frank Coe. The posse from Seven Rivers returned to Lincoln the next day with their prisoner in tow, confining Frank Coe within a room in "The House." Edgar Walz, attempted to keep the men out of the building but was overwhelmed by their numbers.[9] Unknown to the posse, members of the regulators, including Frank Coe's cousin, George, were already in town, hiding among allies at the Ellis Store. A gun battle ignited in town that continued for most of the day until soldiers from Fort Stanton arrived and ended the violence. During the fight, Wallace Olinger (brother of Bob Olinger) reportedly released Frank Coe, gave him a pistol, and told him to run for it. Coe obliged, reuniting with his cousin and the other Regulators at the Ellis Store.

On June 10th, 1878, *J.J. Dolan and Company*, realizing they could not pay Catron or the First National Bank back, signed over the deed to their store and associated land. With Dolan and Riley out of the picture, Catron and Walz continued running the Lincoln store while awaiting another buyer to come forward. Walz also took over duties as postmaster in Lincoln, suggesting the Post Office remain within the old Murphy-Dolan store for the time being.

In July 1878, the Lincoln County War came to a bloody head when the forces of Dolan and Riley collided in Lincoln with those of Tunstall and McSween, during what would be called the Five-Day Battle. During this confrontation, dozens of men vied for control of the town while attempting to arrest those on the other side of the feud. During the fight, the former *J.J. Dolan and Company* store remained eerily vacant and silent. Walz and rancher David M. Easton remained in the building during the battle. On July 19th, Easton witnessed Colonel Nathan Dudley enter the town from the west along with a contingent of soldiers from Fort Stanton. July 19th proved to be the last day of the battle and by 9:00 pm that night, the shooting had stopped. The men in the "The House" did not know it then, but Alexander McSween and at least four other men lay dead around the smoldering ashes of McSween's home. Shortly after 9:00 pm, a group of men approached the store and demanded entry. When Easton and Walz investigated, they discovered the men

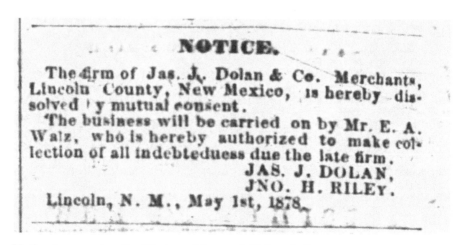

NOTICE.

The firm of Jas. J. Dolan & Co. Merchants, Lincoln County, New Mexico, is hereby dissolved by mutual consent.

The business will be carried on by Mr. E. A. Walz, who is hereby authorized to make collection of all indebtedness due the late firm.

JAS. J. DOLAN,
JNO. H. RILEY.

Lincoln, N. M., May 1st, 1878.

Notice Announcing the Closing of James J. Dolan & Co.
The Weekly New Mexican, July 13 1878

belonged to Sheriff George Peppin's posse along with the body of slain Deputy Robert Beckwith. Easton and Walz allowed the posse to place the body inside the store until the Army moved it to Fort Stanton for burial on the orders of Lieutenant Colonel Nathan Dudley.[10]

With no property left to their name, *J.J. Dolan and Company* dissolved on May 1, 1878, more than two months prior to the climatic end of the Lincoln County War.[11] L.G. Murphy succumbed to his cancer in October 1878 and was buried with full military honors at the Fort Marcy post cemetery, designated a National Cemetery in 1885. With a hefty mortgage hanging over their heads, Dolan and Riley searched for an opportunity to offload their financial liabilities. Their salvation arrived in the form of Will Dowlin and John C. Delaney, post traders at Fort Stanton. On December 21, 1878, *Will Dowlin and Company* purchased Dolan and Riley's interests in "The House" for $3,000. In January 1879, Thomas Catron transferred the mortgage on the building to *Will Dowlin and Company*, who officially occupied the building in the same month.[12] In just a few months, the once-great firm built by L.G. Murphy had disintegrated, their patriarch had died, and "The House" was theirs no more.

Will Dowlin was the brother of Captain Paul Dowlin and partner in his namesake mill located on the Rio Ruidoso. After his brother's murder in 1877, Will took control of their businesses, including the Post Trader position at Fort Stanton, which Paul had filled after the Army had evicted *L.G. Murphy and Company* from the post.[13] Will Dowlin's partner at Fort Stanton was John C. Delaney, and together they formed the company *Will Dowlin and Company*. Unfortunately for Dowlin and Delaney, their business fate in Lincoln was no different from that of Dolan and Riley. In December 1880, the firm went bankrupt and sold the building and associated forty acres to the Lincoln County Board of Commissioners for $15,000.00.[14] Dowlin and Delaney's downfall likely stemmed, at least in part, from the large mortgage debt they assumed from Dolan and Riley. Lincoln County finally had its first permanent government structure—but Billy the Kid's violent escape would soon overshadow the excitement of progress.

PART II

LAW AND ORDER

CHAPTER FIVE
A NEW ERA

In January 1881, county officials began moving into the new courthouse —four months before Billy the Kid's escape from the building. Probate Clerk Ben Ellis and Sheriff Patrick Floyd Garrett moved into their new offices early in 1881, but the remainder of the county officials slowly took their time over the next several months to occupy the building. [1] Sheriff Garrett, elected in November of 1880, made his office in L.G. Murphy's former sitting room, spending $266.50 of county funds to furnish the space in February 1881.[2] Probate Clerk Ellis inhabited the room at the northeast corner of the first floor, operating both the post office and his office from the small space. James Dolan's former bedroom served as the county armory.

In March 1881, County Commissioners voted to build a detached jail on the property. Lincoln's first county jail, or *Carcel*, constructed in 1877 by George Peppin, was located on the east end of town. This first crude jail consisted of a large, log-lined pit, over top of which was a small adobe structure divided into to two rooms—one to cover the hole and one to shield the jailer from the elements.[3] The Lincoln County Commission awarded a $5,560.00 contract to construct the new jail to former owner Will Dowlin.[4] Dowlin had barely started construction on the new building when Garrett arrived in Lincoln on April 21, 1881, with Billy the Kid in tow. With no proper jail, Garrett confined him to the northeast room on the second floor of the new Courthouse. Seven days later, Billy escaped, violently reinforcing the need to finish construction on the purpose-built jail.

The story of Billy the Kid's violent escape from the Lincoln County Courthouse began three years before his arrival back in Lincoln in chains. On April 1, 1878, Billy the Kid and five other Regulators ambushed and killed Sheriff William Brady and Deputy George Hindman on the street in front of the Tunstall Store in Lincoln. Billy was involved in the gunfight at Blazer's Mill three days later, where the Regulators shot and killed Andrew "Buckshot" Roberts. After evading capture for almost three years, Sheriff Garrett apprehended Billy the Kid northeast of Fort Sumner on December 20th, 1880. Garrett transported Billy to Santa Fe, where he remained until March when Deputy Marshals Bob Olinger and Tony Neis transferred him to Mesilla

William Brady
Lincoln County Historical Society

for trial. A jury found Billy guilty of the murder of Sheriff Brady. Judge Warren Bristol sentenced him to death by hanging. Since Billy had committed his alleged crimes in Lincoln County, Bristol ordered officials to transfer him to Lincoln for execution. An escort that included J.W. Bell, Bob Olinger, Billy Matthews, Dona Ana County Sheriff Dave

Tony Neis (L) and Bob Olinger (R), c.1881
Lincoln County Historical Society

Woods, and John Kinney delivered Billy to Lincoln County Sheriff Pat Garrett at Fort Stanton. Garrett then personally transferred Billy the remaining way to Lincoln. Billy arrived at the Courthouse on April 21st, twenty-two days before his scheduled execution.

While awaiting construction of the jail, Garrett confined Billy to the northeast corner room on the courthouse's second floor—coincidentally, L.G. Murphy's former bedroom. The room was accessible only by passing through Murphy's former sitting room, now Garrett's office. The sheriff insisted that Billy the Kid be shackled and handcuffed at all times and guarded twenty-four hours a day by deputies Bob Olinger and J.W. Bell. In addition to Billy the

Kid, Garrett and his deputies held five other prisoners under guard in the Courthouse. Garrett separated these five men—accused of murdering a Sheriff's Deputy and a member of his posse in Dona Ana County—keeping them locked in the room across the hall from Billy.

By all accounts, Billy the Kid, Bell, and Garrett maintained a cordial relationship considering the situation. Bell took his job guarding Billy seriously, as he had been a friend of James Carlyle—the posse member killed during the siege at the Greathouse Ranch involving Billy and his gang on November 27, 1880. A friend of Billy's, John Meadows, later claimed that the outlaw had told him after his escape that he held no hard feelings against Garrett and that the lawman had treated him fairly after capturing him at Stinking Springs. Billy the Kid's history with Bob Olinger differed, as the two had been on opposite sides of the Lincoln County War. According to Meadows, Olinger tormented the young man during his incarceration.

The following six days came and went, accompanied by very little excitement. Billy the Kid spoke to his jailers at length, including with Garrett, and reportedly even played cards with J.W. Bell. The group settled into a routine, and Billy undoubtedly noticed every detail. On April 27th, Sheriff Garrett fatefully decided to leave Lincoln and travel to White Oaks to collect taxes—leaving Billy alone with only two guards. Garrett

Patrick F. Garrett
Lincoln County Historical Society

Gottfried Gauss
Lincoln County Historical Society

allowed the other five prisoners to move around the property, sometimes without an escort, and take their dinner across the street at Sam Wortley's restaurant.

At the time of Billy's incarceration, Gottfried Gauss lived in a small house behind the courthouse, along with Sam Wortley. Although written down ten years later, Gauss's memories of that day's events are one of the only eyewitness accounts available. At about 5 pm on Thursday, April 28th, Bob Olinger escorted the other five prisoners across the street for dinner at Sam Wortley's hotel and restaurant. Just before Olinger left the courthouse, Probate Clerk Ben Ellis and a friend (possibly Michael "Mickey" Cronin) left Ellis' office and headed east towards Isaac Ellis' home for dinner. The business day was over, leaving Billy and Deputy Bell alone inside the building. Billy would never have a better chance at escaping than he did at that moment—the time to act had come.

What exactly happened between Billy and Bell following Olinger's departure is still one of the greatest mysteries of the old west. There are several theories as to what occurred based on Billy's admission given to John Meadows a few days after his escape, the eyewitness account of Gottfried Gauss, and the investigation conducted by Garrett after the fact. However, the fact remains that only two men were present in the Courthouse that day, and one would not live beyond sunset.

Gottfried Gauss stated that he had just stepped out of his home behind the courthouse and was crossing the yard when he heard a scuffle coming from inside, followed by two gunshots. Almost immediately, Bell stumbled out of the back door and directly into Gauss' arms, where he died instantly. According to Meadows, Billy convinced Bell to take him downstairs, presumably to the privy in the courthouse's backyard. On the way back up the stairs, Billy made his move. Slipping one of his hands from the manacles, Billy turned and struck Bell over the head. With his captor now dazed, Billy grabbed his gun from its holster. Billy told Meadows that he attempted to convince Bell to surrender, but the deputy tried to escape down the stairs. Billy then shot him from the top of the stairs. The coroner's inquiry reported that Bell had a significant wound on his head, consistent with reports that Billy had struck him with his heavy iron manacles. A bullet had struck Bell under the right arm, traveling the width of his upper torso and exiting under his left armpit.

Sheriff Garrett's version of events is slightly different, specifically regarding how Billy acquired a pistol. Garrett's report, and subsequent book, stated that as Billy and

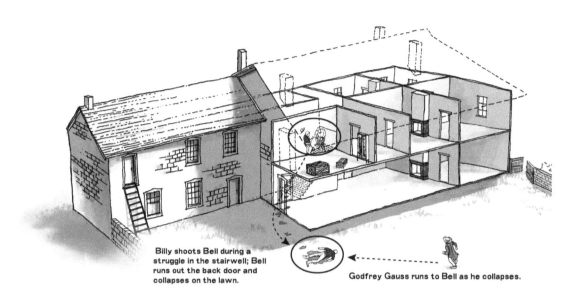

Billy shoots Bell during a struggle in the stairwell; Bell runs out the back door and collapses on the lawn.

Godfrey Gauss runs to Bell as he collapses.

After overpowering James Bell, Billy shoots the deputy likely on the Courthouse staircase. Bell stumbles outside and collapses in front of Gottfried Gauss

Bob Olinger hears the gunshot(s) from across the street and runs from the Wortley Hotel and Restaurant toward the East door of the Courthouse

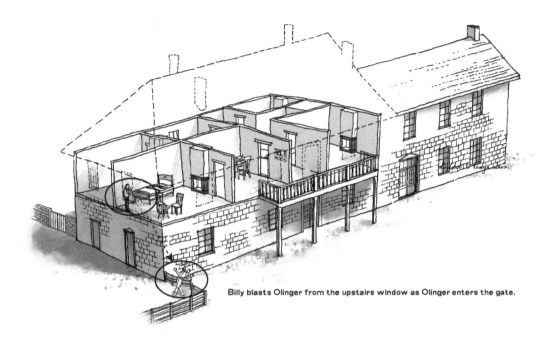

Billy blasts Olinger from the upstairs window as Olinger enters the gate.

From the northeastern window of the Courthouse, Billy ambushes Bob Olinger from the second floor window, firing one barrel of his Whitneyville shotgun, killing him instantly and launching his body back toward the street

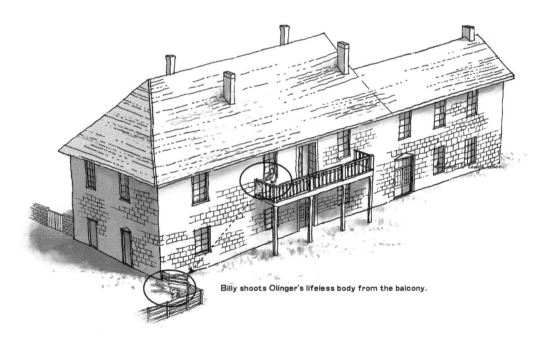

Billy shoots Olinger's lifeless body from the balcony.

Billy exits onto the balcony of the Courthouse and shoots Olinger again with the remaining barrel of his shotgun

Bell ascended the stairs, Billy leaped far ahead of Bell, pushed open the armory door, and retrieved a pistol. He then turned on Bell and shot wildly, only hitting the Deputy because of a fortunate ricochet off the south adobe wall.

There have been other theories regarding how Billy overcame Bell and acquired a firearm. Some reports stated that Billy and Bell were playing cards at the time, and Billy surprised Bell when he reached down to retrieve a card from the floor. Other news articles claimed Bell turned his back on Billy while looking out a window, and the kid attacked him from behind. Regardless, the outcome was always the same—Bell was dead, and Billy was alone in the Courthouse and armed.[5]

One final theory surrounds an unknown accomplice leaving a pistol for Billy in the privy behind the courthouse. This story originates from interviews with A.H. Aguayo, who was ten years old in 1881. In interviews conducted in 1957, Mr. Aguayo stated that a friend of Billy's placed the gun in the privy and then told Billy where it was. Aguayo refused to say who the friend was, but based on statements made by other townspeople, Yginio Salazar is the most likely character. No other evidence has ever surfaced to help substantiate this claim.[6]

The time between Olinger leaving the Courthouse and Billy shooting Bell could not have been more than a few minutes at most. Olinger had just reached his table at the Wort-ley Hotel when he heard the gunshot coming from the direction of the Courthouse. He jumped from his seat and raced across the street towards the gate east of the Courthouse—his destination most likely being the door to the post office. Right as Olinger came through the gate, Gauss rounded the southeast corner of the building and came within a few feet of Olinger. A visibly shaken Gauss quickly informed the lawman that Billy had shot and killed Bell, but he delivered the information too

Billy the Kid waiting at the Courthouse window for Bob Olinger to approach from the Wortley Hotel

late. A voice from above caught Olinger's attention, and he looked up to see Billy standing at the open second-floor window holding his own ten-gauge Whitneyville shotgun. Billy did not hesitate, pulling the trigger and sending a hail of lead tearing through Olinger's chest and head, killing him instantly and sending his body flying back toward the gate. Billy calmly walked out to the balcony and leveled the shotgun at Olinger's lifeless body, adding insult to injury and nine more buckshot into his old enemy. Billy then broke the weapon over the railing and threw it towards Olinger's mangled corpse.

With no lawmen standing in his way, Billy turned his attention to the shackles binding his feet. He announced to all who could hear him that he was now in control and would harm no one unless they stood in his way. Billy demanded something to remove his shackles, and Gottfried Gauss tossed him a miner's pick through a window. He also ordered Gauss to saddle a horse for him while he attempted to liberate his legs.

After almost an hour of labor, Billy only managed to free one of his legs and tucked the remaining chain into his belt. Gauss reappeared with County Clerk Billy Burt's horse, and Billy gathered a few pistols and rifles. As he mounted the horse, his shackles spooked the animal, and the Kid was thrown to the ground, watching as the frightened animal galloped off towards the Rio Bonito. One of the other five prisoners, Alex Nun-

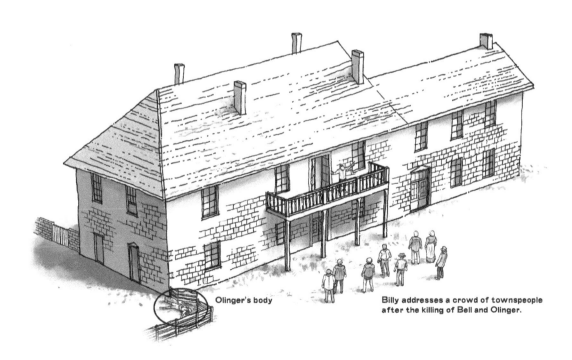

Olinger's body

Billy addresses a crowd of townspeople after the killing of Bell and Olinger.

nely, retrieved the horse while Billy dusted himself off. Once reunited with his vehicle to freedom, Billy remounted and trotted off towards the western sky, reportedly whistling a tune as he completed his final escape from justice. Billy spent the next seventy-eight days on the run but remained in New Mexico. On July 14, Sheriff Garrett and Deputies John W. Poe and Thomas "Kip" McKinney tracked Billy to Fort Sumner, where Garrett shot and killed the outlaw in the doorway of Pete Maxwell's bedroom.

County officials were understandably embarrassed by how simple it was for the most notorious outlaw in New Mexico to escape from their courthouse. Less than two months after Billy the Kid's escape, the County Commissioners reviewed the plans Dowlin submitted for the jail and instructed the clerk to, "Notify Will Dowlin of Fort Stanton, NM, that he is not building the county jail in Lincoln according to contract and that the said board will not accept the labor as performed for the reason aforesaid."[7]

While Dowlin worked on the detached jail, the commissioners needed a temporary space to hold county prisoners. Builders constructed a partition wall in the middle of the rear warehouse to split the room and create a smaller area for prisoners.[8] It is unclear why completing the simple design took so long, and Dowlin or his agents, including Frank Lesnet and S.S. Terrel, appeared before the County Commission at more than one meeting to request extensions to their contract.[9] After numerous delays and extensions, Dowlin finally completed the new prison in January 1882.[10]

While Dowlin toiled away constructing the jail, the County Commission—consisting of Chairman W.W. Paul and members Isaac Ellis, and A.J. Lawton—turned their attention to the interior of the building and other needed improvements.[11] In 1881, the commission paid White Oaks-based contractors James S. Redman and William Nickey $341.00 to convert the billiard room into a courtroom and to add an exterior staircase on the east side of the second-floor balcony. During this conversion of the westernmost room, Redman and Nickey most likely added the interior door allowing access to the room from inside the main building. Redman and Nickey finished their contract on time, completing the job to the Commissioners' satisfaction by June 1st, 1881.[12] The work must have included additional elements not initially contracted for, as the commission paid $410.00 to Redman and Nickey, $60 more than the original amount agreed upon.[13]

In August 1881, the County Commission also awarded a $587.00 contract to William Littell to paint the Courthouse's interior, glaze the windows, repair the wooden doors and window frames, and dig a new well behind the courthouse to supply water to the detached jail.[14] Littell decided to utilize prisoner labor for the well-digging job, specifically the "murderers of old man Obea."[15] Littell and the prisoners finished digging the well, and Littel received his payment. In November 1881, the County Commission paid jailer and former Justice of the Peace John B. Wilson $30 in county scripts to improve Littel's well by lining the shaft with stone.[16] Littel and Wilson completed their work on the well by the spring of 1882 when the Commissioners ordered Ben Ellis to order a pulley for the new water source from Las Vegas. It is uncertain whether Ellis completed this task because the Commission removed him as Probate Clerk during the same meeting, accusing him of chronic absenteeism.[17] The commission's accusations were accurate, as Ben Ellis had recently left Lincoln to marry Ms. Ella Murphy and spend an extended honeymoon in Arizona.

Ruidoso N. M. May 1, 1883.
The firm of Dowlin & Lesnet has this day dissolved partnership, by mutual consent. The business hereafter will be carried on by Frank Lesnet, at Ruidoso, formerly Dowlin's Mills. All parties having accounts with Dowlin & Lesnet will please settle same with Frank Lesnet.

WILL DOWLIN.
FRANK LESNET.

Will Dowlin sold his mill and business to his partner Frank Lesnet in 1883, amid a series of business lawsuits and financial troubles. He died in 1884 at the Colorado State Insane Asylum.
The Lincoln County Leader
White Oaks, New Mexico, Saturday, May 05, 1883
National Archives and Records Administration

CHAPTER SIX
NEW TENANTS

The county found it challenging to occupy all of the space in the large building with official offices—illustrated during a commission meeting held in November 1882, when the commissioners ordered former jailer John B. Wilson to turn in his keys and ensure that "all vacant rooms in said courthouse be locked and securely fastened."[1] Since the building had room to spare, the commission elected to rent space in the courthouse to several private businesses and individuals and sell or lease some excess land surrounding the building. Tenants occupied portions of the building as early as April of 1881 when Gottfried Gauss and Sam Wortley occupied one of the structures behind the building as a home.[2] In October 1881, the Commissioners ordered Probate Clerk Ben Ellis to collect rent from the lessees or have them vacate the premises—perhaps referring to Gauss and Wortley.[3] Despite their difficulty collecting rent, the County Commission leased two rooms to lawyer L.H. Clements in November 1881 for $5.00 monthly. It is unclear exactly what other businesses or individuals leased the premises during the first year the county owned the building. Evidence does suggest that Michael "Mickey" Cronin operated a store from the building at the time of Billy the Kid's escape. "Colonel" Cronin, as he was locally known, shared a long history with the courthouse both as a tenant and while serving in various elected and appointed county positions throughout the 1880s and 1890s.

In May 1883, the new Sheriff of Lincoln County, John William Poe, moved into the building with his wife, Sophie. The Poes rented the rooms "intended for the sheriff," located on the eastern half of the second floor.[4] These included the space previously occupied by Pat Garrett and the room that held Billy the Kid two years earlier. Memories of Billy's escape from Lincoln still reverberated throughout the community of Lincoln, and Sophie Poe grimly reminisced how J.W. Bell's blood was still visible in the stairwell when she and John moved in.[5] The Poes lived in the Courthouse for a little more than one year, relocating in early 1884 to John Poe's newly established VV Ranch between Fort Stanton and Ruidoso.[6] During their time in the building, Sophie Poe transformed the small rooms into a home, furnishing them with goods purchased from Las Vegas, New Mexico and delivered to Lincoln by Isaac Ellis.[7] In her autobiography, Sophie Poe described their new furnishings.

Sophie Poe, c.1885
Lincoln County Historical Society

I felt proud of our bedroom suite, made of black walnut, the bed high and massive, the washstand and bureau equipped with heavy white marble tops. The carpet was a Brussels, with a pattern showing roses. The windows were curtained with white lawn material. This equipment was considered the last work in bedroom furnishing in those days. As a matter of fact, we were considerably ahead of the rest of the community, for few homes in the place could equal the elegance of our bedroom in its furnishings.[8]

In January of 1883, Isaac Ellis received approval from the County Commission to lease the two large rooms in the center of the building as a store for $300.00 per year.[9] Although Ellis held the official lease with the county, "Mickey"

John Poe, c.1900
Lincoln County Historical Society

Cronin continued to operate the store and live on the first floor.[10] Ellis leased a portion of the south room back to the county the following year for temporary use as a classroom. At the same time, the Lincoln County Board of Education constructed a permanent building (now the Lincoln Community Church) to the east of the Courthouse.[11] Ellis, by that time a member of the County Commission, negotiated a lower rent payment for 1884, reducing the price to only $200 per year.[12] In 1885, Ellis elected to move his mercantile business to another location in Lincoln.

—GO TO—

ISAAC ELLIS' NEW STORE

HE KEEPS A SUPPLY GENERAL

Merchandise.

GROCERIES,	DRY GOODS,
CLOTHING,	CARPETS,
BOOTS,	SHOES,
HATS,	CAPS,
SEEDS,	SHEETINGS.

—AND—

FARM IMPLEMENTS.

☞ Will take grain, hides, pelts, wool and all kinds of marketable produce in exchange for goods at the COURT HOUSE,

Lincoln. - - N. M.

Advertisement of Issac Ellis' Store in the Courthouse, managed by Mickey Cronin
Golden Era Lincoln, New Mexico, Thursday, October 09, 1884

Following Ellis' move, the county leased the storerooms and mercantile area to the wife of saloon owner Rocco Emilio, Rosa Esperanza, for $300 per year. Esperanza also leased the fenced garden area to the west of the building for $25.00 per year with the promise that she would maintain the garden gate and the *acequia* ditch that ran alongside it.[13] After Ms. Esperanza's lease agreement expired, the Board of County Commissioners entered into a series of agreements with "Mickey" Cronin to use the storeroom and warehouse rooms until 1896.[14] Cronin paid only $100 per year for the space, a price undoubtedly influenced by his positions as Probate Judge, County Commissioner, and Cattle Inspector—in addition to his partnership in the mercantile with Tom Brent, brother of County Sheriff James Brent.[15] One of the final tenants in the building during its time as the County Courthouse was lawyer George Barber—the second husband of Alexander McSween's widow, Susan. Barber and McSween divorced in 1891 and George remarried the following year. George Barber was a well-respected territorial attorney and rented an upstairs room in the courthouse for one year between 1901 and 1902.[16]

As Lincoln County's center of government, the Courthouse attracted the attention of at least one of the region's newspapers for use as a headquarters. Throughout the 1880s and 1890s, no less than seven different newspapers operated within Lincoln County—most acting as a mouthpiece for either the Democratic or Republican parties. During the

The grounds of the Lincoln County Courthouse, c. 1886
Lincoln County Historical Society

June 2, 1884, meeting of the Board of County Commissioners, editor Jones Taliaferro and his brother proposed renting two rooms within the courthouse to house the *Lincoln County Era* newspaper office.[17] Taliaferro initially operated his paper from White Oaks, but growing political divisions and accusations of impropriety during his tenure as the city's postmaster pushed him to move his operation to Lincoln. Taliaferro benefited from his insider knowledge of county business as the County Probate Clerk and gleaned additional content for his paper by proximity to political decision-makers.

The *Lincoln County Era* was a Democratic-slanted periodical, and its rival, the *Lincoln County Leader,* favored the Republican party. Taliaferro filled the paper with local political news and editorials, often sparring with his rivals, accusing each other and their respective parties of all maleficence and unethical conduct. In November 1885, the citizens of Lincoln County elected James Dolan—former owner of the courthouse building—as their new County Treasurer.[18] Dolan moved into the courthouse office alongside Probate Clerk Jones Taliaferro and, in 1885, purchased the *Lincoln County Era*, changing the name to the *Lincoln Independent*. Dolan continued operating the paper from the courthouse office until November of 1886, when the county leased the space to Moses Wiley, to whom Dolan had sold the newspaper.[19]

The spacious interior of the courthouse was not the only valuable asset the Board of County Commissioners gained when they purchased the property in 1880. The county acquired approximately forty acres surrounding the structure along with the building. During their meeting on October 2, 1882, the Board of County Commissioners voted to sell two and one-half acres of land north of the road and courthouse to Asbury Hope Whetstone for $20 per acre.[20] A rising star in Lincoln County, A.H. Whetstone was a native of Louisiana, a graduate of Louisiana State University, and the brother-in-law of Frank Lea—brother of Roswell founding father Captain Joseph Lea.[21] Whetstone served as a government surveyor, school board officer in Roswell, and General Land Office official during his time in Lincoln County. It is unclear what he intended to use the land in Lincoln for.[22] In April 1883, White Oaks-based attorney George T. Beall purchased two acres of land from the county directly north of the Courthouse on the other side of the public road. Following the purchase, Beall informed the *Lincoln County Leader* that he intended on

The Lincoln County Courthouse, c. 1886. Sheriff James Brent in center with hat in hand. Will Dowlin's 1881 jail is also visible behind the building.
Lincoln County Historical Society

constructing a building that very summer—presumably to house his law practice which he headquartered in Lincoln until the 1890s.[23]

The acreage to the east and west of the building also brought money into the county coffers through agricultural leases. In 1886 the county leased the land west of the courthouse, previously worked by Rosa Esperanza, to *Lincoln Independent* owner Moses Wiley for five years.[24] Civil War Army veteran Moses Wiley—known locally as "Major" Wiley—also briefly practiced law in Lincoln before moving to Tularosa, where he served as Mayor and U.S. Land Commissioner there in the early 1890s.[25] Major Wiley moved further west into Arizona, where he mysteriously disappeared.[26] The year after the county leased the west garden area to Wiley, the commissioners agreed to also rent the eastern acreage to former Probate Clerk Jones Taliaferro for $12.50 per year for five years.[27]

Between 1881 and 1913, the Courthouse also served the community of Lincoln as a meeting space for civic and political organizations. On March 1, 1883, a group of local stockmen met at the Courthouse to create a permanent regional stock association. The meeting, attended by many prominent community members, including John Lea, Sheriff John Poe, James Dolan, and Patrick Garrett, led to the creation of the *Lincoln County Stock Association of New Mexico*.[28] Both major political parties also utilized the space for meetings throughout this period, meeting to elect delegates to statewide conventions and gathering to nominate candidates for local office.[29] In November 1886, the Commissioners rented the facility to Lincoln Lodge #7 of the Knights of Pythias fraternal organization for two years. The only stipulation to this agreement was that the Lodge had to provide the room for

(L to R) Lawmen Patrick F. Garrett, James Brent, and John W. Poe
Lincoln County Historical Society

meetings of the Grand Jury.[30] At this time, the county likely added an interior doorway between the eastern and western rooms on the second floor.

One of the most well-attended events held at the Courthouse during the 1880s was the wedding celebration of Sheriff James Brent and Carlota Baca. James Richardson Brent was born in 1847 and drifted west after serving in the famed Confederate Colonel John S. Mosby's "Ranger" Battalion during the Civil War. Brent lived in White Oaks in November of 1880 when Billy the Kid, "Dirty" Dave Rudabaugh, and others rode into town. Brent joined J.W. Bell, Jim Carlyle, and others as part of the posse that tracked Billy and the gang to the Greathouse Ranch and later served as a Deputy Sheriff under Pat Garrett and John Poe before winning the Sheriff's election in November 1885. Carlota Baca was born at Fort Stanton in 1865 to Saturnino and Juana Baca and raised in Lincoln. Her father, Saturnino Baca, was a decorated Civil War veteran, territorial legislator, Lincoln County Probate Judge, and pillar of the Lincoln community. Following the wedding mass held at the newly consecrated *La Iglesia de San Juan Bautista* in Lincoln, the wedding party gathered in the former billiard room at the Courthouse for dinner and an evening of dancing attended by all of the prominent citizens of Lincoln and White Oaks.[31]

CHAPTER SEVEN
JUSTICE

The Courthouse building served the Lincoln community in multiple ways for more than 30 years. Despite the multitude of uses, the building's primary function was always the location from which county officials administered law and order. Between 1881 and 1913, every sheriff of Lincoln County kept their office in the courthouse in Lincoln. Pat Garrett and John Poe occupied offices on the second floor. James Brent moved his office to the first-floor room previously used as the billiard hall, but officials again moved the office upstairs sometime in the late 1890s or early 1900s. In addition to the Sheriff and his Deputies, the probate judge and probate clerk also made their offices on the courthouse's first floor. The district court met in Lincoln twice a year, once in the fall and once in the spring. The grand and *petit* juries, selected from among the citizens of Lincoln County, made recommendations for indictments in criminal cases. The grand jury also audited county finances and assets once per year. Criminal cases ranged from petty theft to capital murder, and at least two instances resulted in the district judge handing down death sentences to those found guilty. When court was in session, Lincoln came alive. Citizens focused on legal proceedings at the Courthouse during the day but reveled in social activity across the town in the evenings.[1]

Violence in Lincoln County had not simply disappeared after the end of the Lincoln County War, and in 1886 two very different murder cases came before the district court in Lincoln. In the first case, a jury found a twenty-year-old man named William James Bolt, Jr. guilty of murdering another man named Denham (first name unknown).

Bolt was born in Mason County, Texas, and moved west to work cows along the Pecos. According to his confession, the young Texan killed his fellow cowboy because he was confident that Denham was planning to kill him after refusing to participate in a series of planned crimes. Fearing for his life, Bolt ambushed his adversary on the trail, shooting him in the back. Bolt turned himself over to authorities, but his self-defense claim did not convince the jury that he was

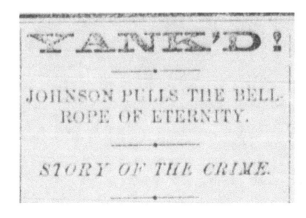

The Headline from DeWitt Johnson's Execution
The Lincoln County Leader
White Oaks, New Mexico, November 27, 1886

innocent of premeditated murder. During an interview at the jail in Lincoln, Bolt confessed that he now believed the man who had told him Denham wanted him dead, fabricated the story as revenge for Denham sleeping with his wife.[2]

In the second case, the jury found DeWitt C. Johnson guilty of murdering Alfred H. Howe during a botched robbery at South Fork near the Mescalero Agency. Johnson and an accomplice, Ernest G. Graves, attempted to rob Howe's home in June of 1886, but the man awoke—shooting Graves in the neck before Johnson shot and killed Howe. South Fork residents soon discovered Howe's body, and a posse caught up with Johnson and the wounded Graves near La Luz, New Mexico. During the October term of court in Lincoln, a jury found Graves guilty of fifth-degree murder, and the judge sentenced him to ten years in the state prison. Despite admitting the crime, the judge showed no mercy to DeWitt Johnson, sentencing him to death.[3]

The Lincoln County Commission paid carpenter Elisha Orr to construct the gallows for William Bolt's execution and he erected the structure in the yard behind the courthouse.[4] By order of the District Judge, Sheriff Brent scheduled Bolt's execution for Friday, June 18, 1886, at 2 pm. Bolt himself, committed to his fate, requested the time moved up—so, at 1 pm, Sheriff Brent entered Bolt's cell and read him the death warrant. Witnesses, including parish priest Father John Garnier, reported that Brent took no pleasure executing his duties and even seemed visibly saddened by the affair. A large crowd gathered around the gallows within the corral of the Courthouse as more spectators leaned from the multiple windows on the building's south side. Sheriff Brent and Father Garnier escorted the prisoner through the crowd, up the stairs, and onto the gallows. Brent pinioned Bolt's arms behind his back and placed a hood over his head. Father Garnier whispered words of encouragement into the young man's ear, and the local newspaper reported his last words to be "God bless you—goodbye all." Sheriff Brent then pulled the lever, and Bolt dropped more than six feet through the trapdoor, his neck breaking at the end of the plunge. After eighteen minutes, the coroner pronounced Bolt dead, and deputies lowered his body and placed him into a simple wooden coffin. The deputies then escorted the casket to the cemetery at the outside of town and swiftly buried the accused murderer with little ceremony[5]

Five months later, on Friday, November 19, 1886, a crowd, reported to be more than 250 people, gathered again behind the courthouse, this time to watch the execution of DeWitt Johnson. Johnson's hanging differed from Bolt's in that Sheriff Brent chose more than nineteen men to serve as deputies—to line the short path from the jail to the gallows. The selected deputies included former Regulator Yginio Salazar, the Sheriff's brother Thomas Brent, and future New Mexico Territorial Governor George Curry. The *Lincoln County Leader* reported that Johnson choked up when asked to provide his last words, but after some whispered advice from Sheriff Brent, Johnson addressed the crowd, saying:

> *It looks hard to hang a man, and yet I know it's the law. Let all young men take my fate as a warning against bad company, which has brought me to this. I am very sorry for what I have done, and if I could, I would do anything for the man I killed. But only God can help him now, and I hope he has helped him, and I hope he will have mercy on me. I hope we will meet in another world and that God will forgive me for what I have done.* [6]

Following Johnson's last words, Sheriff Brent blindfolded him and placed the noose over his neck. He returned to his position beside the lever and told the prisoner "goodbye." The trapdoor opened, and Johnson fell six feet just as Bolt had. After nearly twenty minutes, Dr. Paden from White Oaks pronounced him dead, and the sheriff cut the rope. While the deputies loaded Johnson's body into a coffin, Dr. Paden examined the body, discovering that his neck had not broken as Bolt's had and that he died slowly from strangulation. At 2 pm, Sheriff Brent and several deputies loaded the coffin into the back of a wagon and buried Johnson in the cemetery at the east end of town.

Although only two legal executions occurred at the Courthouse in Lincoln, frontier justice was not uncommon. In January 1883, a civilian named William S. Pearl engaged in a drunken brawl while drinking with soldiers at Fort Stanton. The altercation escalated, and Pearl killed an enlisted man named Downey.[7] The soldier's friends immediately subdued the murderer and would have killed him on the spot had several of the fort's officers, including the post's commander Major Van Horn, not intervened. Van Horn ordered Pearl transferred to civilian authorities in Lincoln to ensure his safety.[8] Two nights later, a dozen soldiers from Fort Stanton made the eight-mile trip to Lincoln and busted down the jail door. The men forced Pearl from his cell and hung him from a nearby tree. The lynch mob did not linger in Lincoln and headed back to Fort Stanton while several other prisoners escaped through the recently destroyed jail door. Sheriff Poe eventually apprehended two of the prisoners, while the rest turned themselves back in rather than face additional criminal charges.[9]

The county incarcerated hundreds of prisoners at the Courthouse between 1881 and 1913, and Billy the Kid was not the only one who successfully escaped custody. In January 1884, Nicolas Aragon and Jose Cruz de la Tafoya stole several horses in Lincoln County. Sheriff John Poe tracked the criminals down and returned them to the Courthouse in Lincoln for trial. During the spring term of court in 1884, a jury found both men guilty, and Judge Warren Bristol sentenced them to five years of hard labor.[10] The New Mexico Legislature did not authorize the construction of a territorial prison until March 1884, and the new facility did not open until the following year. Before that, the territory transferred all prisoners sentenced to longer prison terms to the federal prison at Fort Leavenworth, Kansas.[11] Territorial officials successfully moved Tafoya to Kansas, but a legal technicality delayed Aragon's transfer from Lincoln. On May 28th, 1884, Aragon escaped the Lincoln jail and headed north toward Colfax County. Governor Lionel Sheldon offered a $200 reward for his capture, and Sheriff Poe dispatched Deputy Jasper Corn to apprehend the horse thief. In October 1884, Aragon ambushed Deputy Corn as the lawman approached the outlaws' home near Chaperito, New Mexico.[12] The fugitive shot and killed the deputy's horse, which collapsed on top of Corn, breaking his leg. Aragon then advanced from his hiding spot, shooting the defenseless and injured man in the bowels, leaving him to die

Deputy Jasper Corn
Lincoln County Historical Society

Deputy Johnny Hurley
Lincoln County Historical Society

in agony.[13] After Deputy Corn's murder, Sheriff Poe organized a posse, including future Sheriff James Brent, and Deputies Johnny Hurley, and Barney Mason.

In January 1885, the posse surrounded Aragon at his home. From the darkness, a series of shots exploded from the house. During this initial barrage of gunfire, one bullet grazed James Brent's head and knocked his hat off, and another struck Deputy Hurley, killing him almost instantly. After a two-day siege, Aragon finally surrendered after running out of ammunition. A Santa Fe County jury acquitted Aragon for the murder of Hurley, citing the fact that no one had witnessed the fugitive fire towards the posse through the dark. Authorities relocated Aragon to Colfax County, where a jury found him guilty of second-degree murder for the killing of Deputy Corn, and a judge sentenced him to life in prison.[14]

In 1905, Lincoln County Sheriff John Owen arrested 23-year-old Rosario Emillio for the murder of a young woman named Antonita Carrillo. Rosario was the son of Lincoln merchant and Italian immigrant Rocco Emillio. Rocco Emillio operated a store and saloon directly across the street from the Courthouse before he died in 1904.[15] During the spring term of court held at the Courthouse in Lincoln, a jury found Rosario guilty of first-degree murder, and Judge Edward A. Mann sentenced him to hang on Friday, June 2, 1906. Emillio's attorney filed an appeal, and authorities moved the young man to the penitentiary in Santa Fe to wait out the appeals process.[16] Emillio's appeal progressed to the territorial Supreme Court, which ultimately upheld the original verdict and sentence.[17] Authorities returned Emillio to Lincoln for execution, but his lawyers succeeded in gaining one more postponement. Rosario's fate now lay in the hands of Territorial Governor Herbert Hagerman as he reviewed letters from the young man's friends and family pleading for a reduction in his sentence to that of life imprisonment. The request came from Rosario's family, accompanied by a petition signed by over one hundred citizens of Lincoln County—including all five jury members responsible for convicting him. As the condemned Rosario Emillio awaited his death from a cell in the county jail, Sheriff Owen oversaw the construction of new gallows behind the courthouse. Little did Owen know that his work Little did Owen

Sheriff John Owen
Lincoln County Historical Society

Gallows erected for the execution of Rosario Emillio prior to his escape in 1907
Lincoln County Historical Society

know that his work would be in vain, as Emillio would never walk up the stairs to the hangman's noose.[18]

In the early morning of Saturday, April 27, 1907, Sheriff Owen guarded the prisoners in the Lincoln County jail. At about 3:00 am, Owen fell asleep and awoke to the sound of laughing from one of the cells. He asked the prisoner why he was so amused, at which point the man told him that Rosario Emillio and another prisoner, accused murderer Florencio Gomez, had escaped. The pair had used a file and saw smuggled into them to cut through the bars of their cell and then removed several adobes from the outer wall of the building to flee justice. Owen raised a posse but failed to track the prisoners down despite days of searching the mountains around Lincoln.[19]

JAIL DELIVERY AT LINCOLN.

Rosario Emillio, Convicted of Murder and Gomez, Charged With Murder, Cut Bars and Escape.

From the Capitan News.

Saturday morning a 'phone message came to Capitan from Lincoln that two prisoners, Rosario Emillio and Francisco Gomez, had made their escape from the Lincoln jail at about three o'clock that morning. Sheriff Owen, who was himself on guard that night, was awakened at a quarter to three, by hearing voices, which he immediately investigated, but no signs of a delivery presented themselves, and he retired, satisfied that he must have been mistaken. Worn out by his vigil he almost immediately fell asleep, from which he was again awakened by someone laughing inside the jail. Upon inquiring the cause of the hilarity he was informed by one of the prisoners that the two mentioned above had just left the jail.

The alarm was at once given, and posses raised to hunt down the escaped prisoners, but the moon had disappeared by this time, and the posses had to await the approach of daylight to strike the trail. At daybreak Gomez's trail was discovered leading over the mountain south of town, and he was trailed as far as the Ruidoso, where no further trace could be found. Emillio was trailed up the creek and into the Capitan mountains where it is claimed that he was seen at some sheep camps, but up to this time no officer has laid hands on him. Sheriff Owen and his deputies have ridden night and day in search of the fugitives, all mountain fastnesses that might afford a hiding place have been explored, all avenues of escape are guarded, and officers throughout the Territory have been advised of the escape, and it is believed that they will be apprehended before they can get out of the country.

The prisoners made their escape by sawing two steel bars of the cell, though an examination showed that part of the work was old. After getting out in the main building an adobe wall was all that remained between them and liberty. Removing some adobes from the wall, they left the precincts of the prison without taking time to say good-bye.

Emillio was sentenced to be hanged, but was awaiting a new hearing by the supreme court, and Sheriff Owen intended to start with him Saturday morning for the penitentiary at Santa Fe.

Gomez was in jail on the charge of murder, and his case would have been heard at the coming term of district court.

The Roswell Daily Record
Roswell, New Mexico, Tuesday, May 07, 1907

CHAPTER EIGHT
HOUSEKEEPING

Maintaining such a large building proved challenging for county officials. Between 1885 and 1909, the County Commission invested significant funding for renovations to the Courthouse. These included the addition of two new records vaults, significant renovations of the eastern rooms on the second floor, and construction of a new adobe jail building.

As the county's population grew, so did the volume of government documents. The County Treasurer and Probate Clerk filed dozens of new tax records, probate documents, land patents, and court dockets every month and desperately needed a secure and organized place to maintain the county's records. At their July 7, 1885, regular meeting, the Board of County Commissioners contracted local builder William A. Littel to build a records vault in the northeast corner room of the first floor.

The Lincoln County Clerks office located on the first floor of the Courthouse. The large vault door installed in 1886 can be seen in the background.
Lincoln County Historical Society

The commission allocated $1,391.50 for construction, providing Littel $300.00 in advance and instructing him to complete the project on or before January 1, 1886.[1] The vault was four feet deep, fourteen feet long, and eight feet tall. The brick walls measured nine inches thick—except along the front of the structure, where the bricks were an astounding twenty-two inches wide.[2] This purpose-built room, constructed entirely of kiln-fired bricks, was secured with a massive vault door purchased from the *Diebold Safe and Lock Company* of Canton, Ohio. The door weighed over 1,200 pounds, and the company shipped the huge fixture by train as far as the coal mining town of Carthage—the closest train station to Lincoln, located nearly 100 miles due west of town. The vault door and casement then made the final eighty-mile trek west to its home in the Courthouse, and the Board of County Commissioners certified the entire project complete on October 5, 1886.[3] Probate Clerk Jonas Taliaferro and County Treasurer James Dolan were the first people to use the new vault.[4]

By the mid-1880s, the county had also outgrown the small makeshift courtroom space in the former billiard room on the ground floor. In July of 1886, the Board of County Commissioners hired contractors Charles Bell and Robert B. Brookshire to remove the room partitions dividing the original living quarters on the second floor and repair the floors and ceiling, plaster the walls, and move all of the courtroom furniture from the first floor to the new space.[5] Bell and Brookshire likely removed the muslin cloth ceiling at this time, renovating the vaulted ceiling now visible in the room.—a fact supported by the county's purchase of two large hanging lamps for the courtroom in 1889, which could not have hung from the original cloth ceiling.[6] The pair also repaired the roof's waterspouts around the building and rebuilt the steps leading to the main first-floor door of the building.[7] In October 1886, the County Commissioners instructed Sheriff James Brent to oversee the completion of the courtroom renovations, including fixing furniture and railings, installing the judge's stand, and more.[8] With the work completed, the first term of court in the new room was most likely the fall district court hearings held in November of 1886.

By 1888, the original jail, constructed by Will Dowlin, was deteriorating rapidly. One concerned citizen wrote the following in the pages of the *Lincoln County Leader*:

> *Our jail is a hog pen in which we, very intelligent and humane people that we are, keep human beings who are charged with a crime but often innocent of the charge; our county offices are unfit for records, and one-half of the court-house*

is idle when every inch of it could be used for county offices and a necessary quarter.[9]

Citizens, including James Dolan and future Governor George Curry, petitioned the county to build a new jail.[10] The Board of County Commissioners solicited proposals for the work, receiving only two bids—one from Krouse and Trotter for the construction of the building and one for the cell doors from the *Paulley Cell Company* of St. Louis. The total project cost was $6,486.76, which the County Commissioners felt was too high.[11] With the project at risk of not being funded, Dolan offered to personally finance the project at 92 ½ cents per dollar with the assurance of repayment through a special tax levy.[12] Krouse and Trotter hired, once again, George Peppin to assist in constructing the new building. The new jail was thirty feet wide and fifty feet long and had three jail cells and a space for the jailer.[13] Krouse and Trotter completed the new prison to the satisfaction of the Board of County Commissioners in January of 1889.

The new jail (center) constructed in 1889, alongside the original jail (left) built by Will Dowlin and Frank Lesnet in 1881. Note the original adobe wall built by L.G. Murphy and Company, in 1874.
Lincoln County Historical Society

County officials now turned to other much-needed improvements on the building. In April 1890, the Board of County Commissioners hired Franklin Pierce Banta to build a new front porch on the building. Besides his carpentry skills, Banta owned the *Corner Saloon* in White Oaks. Banta's work was significant and included adding new stairs on both the east and west sides of the balcony and a roof over the whole structure. Despite these improvements, the age and size of the Courthouse continued to cause issues.

Funding for the required maintenance projects was not always easy to find and came primarily from a $.00025 county tax earmarked for "Courthouse and jail repair."[14] The significant improvements completed between 1885 and 1890 addressed some serious issues; however, the seemingly constant need to spend county tax dollars on repairs for the building did not sit well with every citizen in the county. In 1891, local attorney George Barber petitioned the county, requesting a special election to issue $20,000 worth of bonds for a new courthouse. The petition received the requisite signatures, and the county held an election on July 3rd. The citizens of Lincoln County split over the issue, but they ultimately denied the bond—sparing the Courthouse from abandonment and possible destruction.[15] Now firmly committed to maintaining the building, the Board of County Commissioners turned again to George Peppin, paying him $227.40 in the fall of 1891 to cover the entire exterior with a rough coat of plaster. This project marked the first time the building was stuccoed as the adobe walls had remained uncovered and unprotected since its construction in 1874.

The county continued funding minor structural repairs during the next decade as needed. Then, in 1901 the Board of County Commissioners voted to complete another round of significant renovations. On August 29, 1901, commission members opened the bids for the work, which included the installation of a new shingle roof over the entire building; the placement of new flooring over the old floor in the second-floor courtroom; the addition of two inches of mud under the courtroom floor to deaden noise; the addition of a four-foot by four-foot ventilator in the courtroom ceiling; a new entry porch with stairway and rough board ceiling.[16] The county awarded the contract to Capitan-based contractors Little and Fawcett—responsible for building many of the new structures in the region, including the schoolhouses in White Oaks and Capitan.[17] The firm worked quickly, finishing the project before the fall term of court held in November 1901.[18]

In 1903, the county completed the final significant alteration to the Courthouse building during its period of ownership. Again, needing additional secure space, the Board

The Courthouse, Lower Level
1910

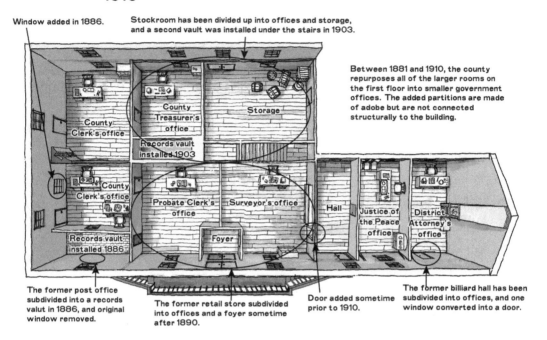

Window added in 1886.

Stockroom has been divided up into offices and storage, and a second vault was installed under the stairs in 1903.

Between 1881 and 1910, the county repurposes all of the larger rooms on the first floor into smaller government offices. The added partitions are made of adobe but are not connected structurally to the building.

County Clerk's office

County Treasurer's office

Storage

Records vault installed 1903

County Clerk's office

Probate Clerk's office

Surveyor's office

Hall

Justice of the Peace office

District Attorney's office

Records vault installed 1886

Foyer

The former post office subdivided into a records valut in 1886, and original window removed.

The former retail store subdivided into offices and a foyer sometime after 1890.

Door added sometime prior to 1910.

The former billiard hall has been subdivided into offices, and one window converted into a door.

The Courthouse, Upper Level
1910

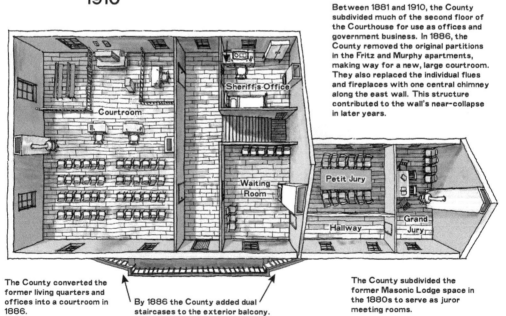

Between 1881 and 1910, the County subdivided much of the second floor of the Courthouse for use as offices and government business. In 1886, the County removed the original partitions in the Fritz and Murphy apartments, making way for a new, large courtroom. They also replaced the individual flues and fireplaces with one central chimney along the east wall. This structure contributed to the wall's near-collapse in later years.

Sheriff's Office

Courtroom

Waiting Room

Petit Jury

Hallway

Grand Jury

The County converted the former living quarters and offices into a courtroom in 1886.

By 1886 the County added dual staircases to the exterior balcony.

The County subdivided the former Masonic Lodge space in the 1880s to serve as juror meeting rooms.

of County Commissioners turned to the trusted original builder of the courthouse building, George Peppin, to construct a new vault under the courtroom and between the north and south rooms of the first floor. The county paid Peppin $145.00 to install the brick vault and contracted with store owner Henry Lutz to procure a vault door, costing $213.00.[19] The county procured the service of master builder Peppin on multiple occasions during their stewardship of the building. At various times, Peppin painted interiors, repaired and plastered adobes, and mended fences—working on the building he helped to design and build until a year before he died in 1904.[20]

In the years following these final significant renovations, the county created additional office space by further partitioning the building. In its last years as a county building, the first floor housed the offices of the District Attorney, Justice of the Peace, County Surveyor, Probate Judge, County Clerk, and County Treasurer—all in separate private rooms. On the second floor, along with the courtroom, the County Sheriff occupied the south central room, constructed initially as James Dolan's bedroom, and the Petit and Grand Juries convened in separate spaces carved out of L.G. Murphy's masonic hall.[21]

Lincoln County Sheriff Charles A. Stevens was the last sheriff to have an office in the Courthouse in Lincoln.
Lincoln County Historical Society

PART III

PRESERVATION

CHAPTER NINE
A HARD FIGHT

The demographics and economics of Lincoln County changed significantly between 1880 and 1900. More and more Anglo settlers moved into the region, bringing new industries, including mining, large-scale cattle ranching, and timber harvesting. Before the 1880s, most Lincoln County residents resided near the agricultural communities along the Bonito and Hondo Valleys. In 1860, around 350 individuals lived in the area surrounding Lincoln, including the Hondo and Ruidoso River Valleys.[1] By 1900, more than 800 people lived in White Oaks alone—with more than half of the household heads working as miners.[2] Then, in 1899, the El Paso and Northeastern Railway extended their established rail line from Alamogordo north to Carrizozo and east to the coal fields near a new town named Capitan.[3] Almost overnight, the populations of Carrizozo and Capitan exploded, reaching more than 1,500 combined residents by 1910.

Meanwhile, Lincoln's population was shrinking as residents moved from their farms to these new population centers. By 1901, citizens in Lincoln County began debating moving the county seat to White Oaks or Capitan. Leaders in White Oaks were even willing to accept a move to Capitan if the El Paso and Northeastern Railway funded the construction of a new courthouse and jail.[4] In 1903, the territorial legislature discussed possibly splitting Lincoln County into two counties. At this point, local discussions began regarding a more centralized county seat should boundaries be moved, with residents suggesting both Carrizozo and Capitan as possibilities.[5] In July 1909, citizens presented a petition—signed by more than 1,200 residents—to the Board of County Commissioners.

The petition requested an election to determine whether Lincoln would remain the county seat or relocate to Carrizozo. The petition met all requirements, and the commissioners set the special election for Tuesday, August 17th, 1901. [6]

There were numerous arguments from both sides regarding why the county should or should not move the seat of power to Carrizozo, with the fate of the old county courthouse in Lincoln chief among them. The cost of building a new courthouse in Carrizozo was at the heart of the arguments. Those in favor of the move argued that repairs on the old building in Lincoln cost taxpayers more than the interest on any bonds issued to construct a new building.[7] The Carrizozo Chamber of Commerce printed nearly daily arguments in the *Carrizozo News* about the benefits of moving county operations from Lincoln. Many of the leading citizens of Lincoln—including Dr. John Laws, merchant J.J. Aragon, and lawyer George Barber—wrote counter editorials leading up to the election.[8]

Ultimately, the simple fact that Carrizozo, and nearby White Oaks, had larger populations was enough to guarantee the move. Following certification of the ballots, county commissioners confirmed that citizens cast 899 votes to move the county seat to Carrizozo and 614 for leaving it in Lincoln—a difference of 285 votes or 18.8%.[9] Unsurprisingly, the smaller communities in the eastern sections of the county voted in favor of Lincoln, while the larger population centers on the western side voted for Carrizozo. In line with state law, Carrizozo became the official county seat as soon as the Board of County Commissioners certified the vote, but the fight over the decision would drag on for four long years.

Immediately following the election, a group of prominent lawyers, led by George Barber and Thomas Catron, filed suit in the district court, arguing that the

CARRIZOZO WINS BY AN OVERWHELMING MAJORITY.

In last Tuesday's election, on the question of the removal of the county seat from Lincoln to Carrizozo, 1513 votes were cast, of which Lincoln received 614 and Carrizozo 899, giving Carrizozo a majority of 285. The official canvass of the vote will be made by the commissioners next Monday; and, as there were only two candidates and little room for confusion, it is believed the official count will correspond with the figures given.

The following table shows the precincts, the number of votes cast and how they were divided:

No.	Name.	Lincoln.	Carrizozo.
1.	Lincoln,	150	16
2.	San Patricio,	149	10
3.	Los Pallas,	77	23
4.	Picacho,	37	2
5.	Raventon,	40	13
6.	Richardson,	16	13
7.	Jicarilla,	14	83
8.	White Oaks.	5	65
9.	Capitan,	68	29
10.	Ruidoso,	36	25
11.	Nogal,	4	57
12.	Bonito,	15	65
13.	Corona,	2	135
14.	Carrizozo,	1	298
15.	Oscuro,	—	65
	Totals,	614	899

Precinct voting tallies from County Seat vote, 1909
Carrizozo Outlook, August 20, 1909

The "New" Lincoln County Courthouse constructed in Carrizozo
Lincoln County Historical Society

vote to move the county seat was illegal because the County Commission failed to appoint a registration board sixty days before the election. On the other side, the County Commission argued that this law did not apply to a special election, ordered to occur sixty days after a petition's presentation. Catron and Barber's argument was weak, but the savvy litigators kept the issue tied up in the district and territorial courts for several years. With no suitable records office or jail yet constructed, the County Clerk, Treasurer, and Sheriff chose to remain at the old Courthouse in Lincoln. Under the advice of the District Attorney, the Board of County Commissioners, Probate Judge, and District Court relocated to a temporary space in Carrizozo.[10]

In March 1910, the Board of County Commissioners awarded a $26,000 contract to Curry County contractor Ben Bechtel for constructing the new courthouse and jail in Carrizozo. Bechtel began construction immediately and had completed half of the building by October 1910. That month, opponents of the move successfully lobbied the Territorial Supreme Court to issue an injunction halting construction.[11] The injunction prevented the county from paying out any further funds for constructing the new courthouse and jail until the courts finalized a decision on the original case. Work ceased, and the building sat unfinished for the next three years. With no facility in Carrizozo, the County Clerk,

Treasurer, and Sheriff remained in the courthouse in Lincoln until the county completed the new building.

While the government in Lincoln remained geographically split, Catron and Barber worked their case through the system, presenting arguments to the territorial supreme court and the new State Supreme Court following New Mexico's admittance as a state on January 6, 1912. Finally, the United States Supreme Court received the case in January of 1913—officially submitted as Gray v. Taylor. On January 20, 1913, Justice Oliver Wendell Holmes, Jr. issued the court's decision, siding with the Board of County Commissioners. Their ruling certified the election as legal and that relocating the county seat from Lincoln to Carrizozo was official and binding.[12] Ben Bechtel resumed work on the Carrizozo courthouse and jail in March 1913, completing the building in September of the same year. Bechtel sued the Board of County Commissioners for monetary damages related to the delays, and Curry County District Judge John T. McClure awarded him $3,750.00 for his troubles.[13] In the fall of 1913, the remaining county officials and staff relocated their offices to the new courthouse in Carrizozo, along with all county records. This move included hauling the massive vault door from Lincoln and reinstalling it at the new courthouse in Carrizozo. The halls of the Courthouse in Lincoln went silent, marking the end of another era for the building.

The Territorial Delegation from New Mexico on the steps of the White House. The group traveled to Washington D.C. to witness President Howard Taft sign the bill establishing New Mexico as a state on January 9, 1912. Among the group was former Territorial Governor and future Courthouse Museum Curator, George Curry (first row, second from right)
Lincoln County Historical Society

The Courthouse stood empty between 1913 and 1919, and the structure deteriorated significantly. The county commission attempted to sell the building into private hands, but no one offered bids above the legal threshold of two-thirds of the building's appraised value. As early as 1917, preservation advocates began calling for restoring the old Courthouse and transforming it into a museum.[14] Lincoln County State

Representative Ira O. Wetmore introduced a bill in the state legislature, recommending that the county convey the old Courthouse in Lincoln to the state for use as a "Museum and repository of the pioneer days of the Southwest." Wetmore's House Bill 117—which also included $10,000 earmarked for the renovation of the Courthouse—passed the house by 40 votes to 3 in February 1917.[15] Despite support for the bill in the House of Representatives, a Senate sponsor never came forward, and the bill died without further debate.

Members of the Lincoln School's basketball team, c.1925. The team played their games on an outdoor court adjacent to the Courthouse building. *Lincoln County Historical Society*

State and county leaders put the Courthouse's transformation into a museum on hold—instead, turning their attention to utilizing the building to support the growing educational needs of the Lincoln community. In October 1919, Lincoln County School District No. 1 offered a solution to the county's challenge of maintaining an empty and deteriorating building. The School Board needed property in Lincoln to build a new schoolhouse, and the Courthouse property to the east of the existing building was a perfect location. In addition to the land for the new construction, the school district would have access to the large Courthouse building itself as additional classroom space, extracurricular activities, storage, and more.[16] The Board of County Commissioners contracted with El Paso-based architectural firm *Trost and Trost* to design the new three-room schoolhouse in Lincoln, awarding the construction contract to Porfirio Chavez.[17]

In 1921, the school district moved the primary classrooms for 4th through 9th grades from the courthouse to the newly constructed building adjacent to the Courthouse on land that was initially part of the eastern garden plots leased to Jones Taliafiero and others. *Trost and Trost* modeled the Lincoln school after a similar school they had recently built in nearby Ancho, New Mexico. The firm's choice of construction material was the defining difference between the two structures. In Ancho, builders used locally fired bricks and chose traditional adobe at Lincoln. The Ancho school also contained one additional room not included in the plans for the structure in Lincoln—a detail that would prove disastrous for the structure in the future.[18] After the new school opened in 1921, the district continued using the former Courthouse as overflow space for the Manual Training Arts programs, Domestic Science classes, and Physical Culture courses.[19] The people of Lincoln also used the ample courtroom space on the second floor for local meetings and events, such as community dances, and the school board installed a platform stage in the room for performances.[20] As the population of Lincoln diminished, the need for additional classroom space also decreased; by the early 1930s, the Courthouse was once again empty and deteriorating.

Structural issues at the empty Courthouse paled in comparison to the Board of Education's problems with the new schoolhouse after they attempted to expand the building in 1935. After starting renovations on May 5, 1935, workers ran into a significant problem after only three days of work. The foundation of the school's rear wall failed, leading to the total collapse of the east side of the structure—nearly crushing several students attending classes inside. Thankfully no one suffered any severe injuries, but the School Board needed a quick solution to their sudden lack of classroom space in Lincoln. Fortunately for the community, the recently established Works Progress Administration provided emergency funding for a new, larger building designed by Roswell architect Dick Garner and constructed by local contractor B.G. Robinson.[21]

Laborers first noticed some major structural concerns at the adjacent Courthouse during the construction of the new schoolhouse. Years of use and renovations on the building took a toll on the physical stability of the structure, specifically along the east wall. The addition of a fireplace during the courthouse years significantly undermined the wall's strength, and visible cracks appeared as the entire face

The east side of the Courthouse supported with wooden braces following the near collapse of the exterior wall. c.1935
Lincoln County Historical Society

buckled under the roof's weight. Later analysis would reveal that the wall was in danger of collapsing at any moment. While the Works Progress Administration worked on the schoolhouse next door, the project's foreman lived in the nearby Courthouse. During his time there, he noticed significant movement along the east wall of the large building. It is also likely that the heavy excavation equipment used at the adjacent schoolhouse work site, also exasperated and accelerated damage to the courthouse walls. He decided that the potential for catastrophic collapse outweighed his need for a place to stay, and he vacated the building rather than risking serious injury or death.[22] The situation was clear—the historic Lincoln County Courthouse was in dire straits and at risk of being lost forever.

Construction of the "new" Lincoln School in 1936 adjacent to the Courthouse. This project, funded by the Works Progress Administration, led to the county completely abandoning the Courthouse building aside from storage.
Lincoln County Historical Society

Front view of the Courthouse, c.1920
Lincoln County Historical Society

Lincoln County Courthouse, c. 1920
Lincoln County Historical Society

Rear view of the Courthouse, c.1927
Lincoln County Historical Society

East side of the Courthouse including Billy the Kid's window, c. 1927
Lincoln County Historical Society

Southwest corner of the Courthouse and west wing, c.1927
Lincoln County Historical Society

(L to R) Photographer W.A. Carrel, Miguel Luna, Maurice Fulton, and Captain Booker c.1927
Lincoln County Historical Society

Photographer W.A. Carrel made several trips to Lincoln during the 1920s. One of his most famous images was a simple photograph of a single chair sitting in front of the window that Billy the Kid shot Bob Olinger from.
Lincoln County Historical Society

CHAPTER TEN
SAVING AN ICON

Roman Maes was born in Lincoln on February 28, 1903. He lived most of his early life in San Patricio but moved back to Lincoln in the late 1920s with his wife, Theodora. The couple purchased a home directly across from the Courthouse, and Roman drove a school bus for the school district.[1] In the late 1920s and early 1930s, Maes witnessed a growth in the number of tourists passing through Lincoln. Along with its convenient location along U.S. Highway 380, this increase in traffic owed itself to a renewed interest in the story of Billy the Kid and the Lincoln County War—fueled by the 1926 book The Saga of Billy the Kid, written by Walter Noble Burns. Maes saw an opportunity, opened a saloon, *La Paloma Bar*, and filled it with relics from the Old West. Maes went one step further and put signs on the abandoned courthouse building, encouraging tourists to explore the building—using a key he kept at his store and museum. One of the many tourists that came through Lin-

Roman Maes and Robert Howard, June 1935
Lincoln County Historical Society

coln during this period included noted pulp fiction author and creator of Conan the Barbarian, Robert E. Howard. In June 1935, Howard and his friend Truett Vinson took a road trip from Texas to Santa Fe, New Mexico, stopping in Lincoln. In a letter to fellow author and friend H.P. Lovecraft, Howard recalled his experience at the Courthouse.

Maes gave us the key to the old courthouse, which was once Murphy's store. It is used as a storeplace for junk now, and there is talk, we were told, of tearing it down to build a community hall. It should be preserved...We
tried to re-create the situation that April morning in 1881 when the Kid, tricking his captor, J. Bell, off-guard by a game of monte, snatched his pistol and fought his way to liberty. We followed the route through the rooms and hallway by which Billy marched his prisoner, intending to lock him into the armory...We stood at the window from which the Kid watched Bob Ollinger run across the street at the sound of the shot; the same window from which he poured eighteen buckshot into Ollinger's breast from the man's own shotgun.[2]

Roman Maes and Robert Howard were not alone in their interest in preserving and promoting the Courthouse as a historic site and destination for tourists. In 1934, the Chaves County Historical and Archaeological Society secured the deed for the old torreon in Lincoln from the State of New Mexico. The group then raised funds and combined them with support from the Federal Emergency Relief Administration and the Works Progress Administration to restore the historic landmark, dedicating it on February 23, 1935.[3] The successful preservation of the torreon encouraged local community members and leaders in Santa Fe and Washington to think more broadly about the future of Lincoln—specifically regarding the old County Courthouse. In early 1937, United States Senator Carl Hatch met with National Park Service leaders to discuss declaring the old courthouse in Lincoln a National Monument.[4] The New Mexico State Senate passed a "Memorial" in February 1937, supporting Hatch's efforts and requesting the Senate Public Lands Committee to consider introducing legislation authorizing the National Park Service to take control of the courthouse and other properties in Lincoln. However, legislators at the federal level responded slowly. Lincoln's state representative, L.P. Hall, told reporters

The torreon prior to restoration
Lincoln County Historical Society

The restored torreon in Lincoln, completed in 1935
Lincoln County Historical Society

for the *Albuquerque Journal* that there was "little likelihood" of action by the federal government regarding the matter but that the discussions were moving ahead with the leaders at the State Museum level. [5]

In 1937, citizens in Lincoln County organized the Lincoln County Society of Art, History, and Archaeology (LCSAHA). Founding members, including Larry H. Dow, L.P. Hall, George T. McQuillen, and George Titsworth, worked with the Assistant Director of the New Mexico History Museum, Dr. Reginald Fisher, to draft bylaws and rules of procedures.[6] From its inception, the LCSAHA maintained an organizational connection to the New Mexico History Museum. Article III of the society's bylaws stated that the group was to "cooperate with the Museum of New Mexico toward the end that a branch of the State Museum may be granted to the society."

Louise Coe was the first woman elected to the New Mexico State Senate (1924) and served Senate Pro Tempore from 1929 until leaving office in 1941
Lincoln County Historical Society

Once established, the new society filled its board of trustees with members from the Lincoln community, well-schooled in the history and culture of the region. These included Wilbur Coe, Albert Pfingsten, John Penfield, and artist Peter Hurd. Ex-officio members of the board included State Senate President Pro Tempore Louise Coe, State Senator Perry Sears, State Representative Hector Johnson, and Dr. Reginald Fisher.[7] During the 13th session of the New Mexico State Legislature, L.P. Hall introduced House Bill 114, "Making the old Lincoln County Courthouse a state museum." Senator Louise Coe sponsored a similar bill on the senate side of the legislature, SJR 6. Coe's legislation recommended "Making a branch of the state museum of the old Lincoln County Courthouse and grounds and designating them as a state monument."[8] The House of Representatives unanimously passed HB 114 on February 16th, 1937, and Governor Clyde Tingley signed the bill into law on February 22, 1937.[9]

The LCSAHA wasted little time assisting in securing state title to the Courthouse and an 89' x 226' lot surrounding it. On May 20th, 1937, the State of New Mexico officially took ownership of the property and building from the Lincoln County Board of Education and, in early 1938, declared the building an official State Monument.[10] With the property secured, the LCSAHA and Museum of New Mexico sought funding and expertise to lead the restoration of the historic building. The museum petitioned the Works Progress Administration (WPA) for funding the extensive preservation work, and in February 1938, President Franklin Roosevelt authorized $8,657.00 for the project.[11]

At the recommendation of Edgar Hewett, Director of the School of American Research and the New Mexico History Museum, the WPA selected Jerome W. Hendron to oversee the physical restoration of the Courthouse. Hendron, a graduate of the University

FDR APPROVES REBUILDING OF LINCOLN JAIL

Plan to Restore Courthouse Where Billy the Kid Made His Escape

By RICHARD COWELL

WASHINGTON, Feb. 7 (AP) — The President has given his approval for an $8657 WPA allotment to rehabilitate the old Lincoln County court house at Lincoln, N. M., which was linked with many of the escapades and legends of the Southwest's picturesque outlaw, "Billy the Kid."

The desperado—some say he slew 21 persons during his bandit career—was jailed in the old building and escaped from it, so one legend goes, to hide at the home of a sweetheart, at Ft. Sumner.

The New Mexico legislature has asked the Federal Government to have the old court house designated a national historical monument. It is one of a number of such places receiving the Interior Department's consideration for such distinction.

Lincoln Court House Being Remodeled to Restore 'War' Touch

ROSWELL, N. M., April 10 (AP)— The historic old court house of Lincoln County, at Lincoln, N. M., is being remodeled under a WPA project, it was announced by Harry Mundell, director.

Under the direction of J. W. Hendron of the State Museum at Santa Fe, workers will seek to restore the old building to as near as possible the same appearance it had during the days of the "Lincoln County War."

Photographs of this period are needed, Mundell announced, so that restoration will be as accurate as possible. Anyone having such photographs is requested to communicate with the local office of the WPA, or with J. W. Hendron, at the State Museum.

The Albuquerque Tribune
Albuquerque, New Mexico,
Monday, February 7, 1938

The Albuquerque Journal
Albuquerque, New Mexico,
Monday, April 11, 1938

of New Mexico and a pupil of Hewett's, had spent several field seasons working as an archaeologist and custodian at Bandelier National Monument. Specifically, the 26-year-old Hendron had worked on restoring several significant kivas for the National Park Service and assisted in developing the agency's "Ruins Restoration Program." Hendron's experience with traditional building methods and historical research made him an ideal candidate for leading the complex project in Lincoln.

Jerome Hendron and his crew of laborers arrived in Lincoln in April 1938. In consultation with the LCSAHA, Hendron and the New Mexico History Museum elected to attempt to restore the Courthouse to its appearance during the Lincoln County War and "to the time when Billy the Kid made his escape, in 1881."[12] Hendron immersed himself in the history of Lincoln, seeking out and interviewing anyone who remembered the courthouse during its earlier years. These interviewees included former regulator George Coe, Mrs. Amelia Bolton Church, whose father, John Bolton, served as Lincoln Postmaster at the courthouse, and Mrs. Lily Casey Klasner—who was engaged to Bob Olinger at the time of his murder.[13] Hendron also placed ads in local newspapers soliciting images of the building detailing what it might have looked like at the time of Billy the Kid's escape—unfortunately, it seems that no new photos surfaced.[14]

George and Phoebe Coe on the West side of the Historic Lincoln County Courthouse, 1939.
Lincoln County Historical Society

CHAPTER ELEVEN
RESTORING AN ICON

On April 6, 1938, Hendron's team began their work. The team ranged between eight and sixteen laborers, not including Hendron and sometimes a WPA truck driver. Hendron employed a diverse group of laborers comprised of men skilled in various construction arts, including masonry, carpentry, roofing, and excavation. The team's first task included cleaning the building and removing the "rubbish, cans, timbers, lumber, boxes, stoves, rags, papers, and coal, and salvaging what was in fair condition." When the school board abandoned the building in 1936, they left most of the furniture and fixtures, and the entire building was filled with discarded material, "knee-deep" in some places, as Hendron described it.[1] At the same time, workers focused on stabilizing the northeast and southeast corners of the building with large timber braces. Once the team cleared and stabilized the building, Hendron could conduct his structural analysis and determine what immediate work he needed to accomplish to stabilize the structure and prepare it for restoration. Following his investigation, Hendron concluded that the building was salvageable but structurally weakened by years of renovations and weather damage from poor drainage. Years of rain and snow melt had also undermined the foundation, which Hendron decided

Jerome W. Hendron
University of New Mexico
"Mirage" Yearbook, 1934

needed immediate repairing and support.

During the first few weeks of restoration work, Hendron and his team removed large amounts of interior plaster from the walls of the building. Much of the interior finishes were in a state of disrepair so advanced that the only option available was to strip the plaster down to bare adobe and start anew. Hendron noted that in some areas, plaster was more than one inch

Broken furniture and debris removed by Jerome Hendron and his crew, 1938.
Lincoln County Historical Society

thick—an indication that workers had applied multiple layers over time in an attempt to prolong the life of the building. Examination of the plaster layers also aided Hendron in determining which interior walls were original to the building, as the oldest components had a base layer of primitive lime *gaspe*, commonly used in territorial period construction.[2] As Hendron and his men worked, they peeled away the timeline of the building, rewarded with a glimpse into the craftsmanship that had gone into its construction sixty-five years earlier under the supervision of L.G. Murphy and George Peppin.

With the interior cleaned and plaster removed, Hendron turned his attention to one of the most critical elements of his work—stabilizing the building's massive foundation. Hendron underpinned the original supports to accomplish this task with new stone quarried from Spring Canyon, two miles northwest of Lincoln.[3] His crew dug trenches, two feet wide and three feet long, around the entire building at five-foot intervals. The troughs extended approximately six to eight inches below the historical foundation, undercutting it by twelve inches.[4] Workers then filled the undercut trenches with the quarried stone and cement (at a four-to-one mix ratio) to the surface, extending two feet beyond the walls. In one spot, along the northwest corner of the building, the crew added one much larger and longer stone "pin." Hendron noted that this corner was the weakest point in the foundation and required additional support to ensure no further settling.[5] To preserve their work on the foundation and to keep the fill dirt from washing away, Hendron designed and constructed a one-hundred-foot-long limestone retaining wall across the entire front of the building, set fifteen feet in front of the building and measuring two feet high and twenty inches wide.

Once completed, Hendron was confident the foundation would no longer sink or spread outward and turned his attention to the rest of the building.[6]

With work on the foundation ongoing during the spring of 1938, Hendron assigned several crew members to make adobe bricks needed for additional structural restoration. The School Board agreed to allow the crew to use part of its adjoining property to produce and stage the needed adobes. The Southern Pacific Railroad donated water and straw for the process, and Hendron sourced sand initially from Carrizozo, transporting it to Lincoln via truck and sifting on location at the Courthouse. However, by late April, locals helped to identify a better source of sand that required no on site screening and was located only fourteen miles from Lincoln. Unfortunately, Hendron left no other directional information regarding where this miracle sand originated. According to Hendron, his crew could "put out better than two-hundred bricks per day if the weather is favorable."[7] The team needed more adobes than initially expected, as structural damage caused by years of neglect, water damage, and careless renovations had resulted in large vertical cracks along the faces of nearly every wall. While stabilizing the walls, Hendron attempted to reuse as many original adobes as possible. Still, the crew ultimately needed to make approximately five thousand new bricks—measuring the exact dimensions as the originals.[8]

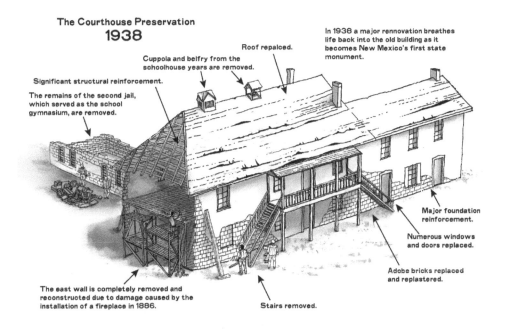

The Courthouse Preservation
1938

Roof repalced.

In 1938 a major rennovation breathes life back into the old building as it becomes New Mexico's first state monument.

Cuppola and belfry from the schoolhouse years are removed.

Significant structural reinforcement.

The remains of the second jail, which served as the school gymnasium, are removed.

Major foundation reinforcement.

Numerous windows and doors replaced.

Adobe bricks replaced and replastered.

The east wall is completely removed and reconstructed due to damage caused by the installation of a fireplace in 1886.

Stairs removed.

Jerome Hendron and his team working on the Courthouse restoration, 1938-1939

In May 1938, Hendron began preparations for stabilizing the failing east wall of the building that had recently concerned a WPA foreman so much that he had refused to stay in the building. With the foundation reinforced, the crew now had the stability they needed to lift the roof ever so gently off the top of the wall to allow the repair and replacement of damaged adobes. Hendron harvested twenty-five-foot Ponderosa pine posts from the nearby Capitan Mountains to build the necessary supports and scaffolding. Due to the high price of lumber and a shortage of tools, Hendron and his crew relied heavily on local community members for assis-

Crews work on the Northeast corner of the Courthouse along the fragile East wall, 1938. The interior bricks from the 1886 vault can be seen as well.
Lincoln County Historical Society

tance in obtaining these materials.[9] Using these massive pine poles on both the interior and exterior of the wall, workers lifted the roof off the wall just one-quarter of an inch—just high enough to allow the removal of the adobe bricks if necessary. Hendron noted that the wall was generally in excellent condition except for the noticeable bulging caused by the non-original chimney. Once the crew lifted the roof and removed the plaster down to the adobes, they discovered large vertical cracks along the northeast and southeast corners of the building, running its entire height.

Hendron determined that the crew needed to remove the east wall to repair and stabilize the structure properly. Fortunately, the team salvaged many of the original adobe bricks, placing them back into the wall as they worked. While the team completed this work, they inserted large metal tie rods through holes drilled in the wall to hold the wall together. The workers fitted these tie rods with turnbuckles so they could adjust them as needed while they removed and replaced the adobe bricks.[10] The windows and door frames on the east side of the building had also distorted and warped as the structure settled over the years, and rain and snow poured down on them. Hendron and his workers carefully removed the original wood windowsills and door jambs, leveled adobes where needed, and placed the fixtures in their original locations. During the project, the crew replaced over two hundred broken window panes around the Courthouse.[11]

Once work commenced on the east wall, Hendron relayed several causes for the delay to his superior in Santa Fe, Dr. Reginald Fisher of the Museum of New Mexico. Specifically, he lamented that they could not remove the entire wall simultaneously for fear that the north and south walls would collapse. He claimed that a lack of equipment slowed the process as "mud and adobes have to be transported to the upper story by manpower."[12] Weather also impeded progress as the seasonal monsoons typical of the Sacramento Mountain region moved into the area in June of 1938, causing delays in work and the loss of many of the adobes already formed and left outside to dry. Hendron relayed an astute observation to Dr. Fisher in a June 25, 1938 report stating, "It is very difficult to do mud work in damp weather."[13] Working through these adverse conditions, the team completed the reconstruction of nearly the entire wall by early July 1938. The only portion remaining undone was the central section where they would build the "new" chimney to replace the one responsible for so much damage.[14] Unfortunately, sourcing flue tile proved more difficult for Hendron than expected, forcing the crew to finish the wall without the chimney with plans to install the feature later—but their small victory over the troublesome wall proved short-lived.[15]

In the end, Jerome Hendron and his group of skilled workers proved no match for the power of Mother Nature. Because of near-constant moisture, the new bricks installed along the east wall of the building failed to dry properly. When the crew removed the Ponderosa pine supports, the still-moist adobes bulged under the roof pressure, windows, door jambs, and older bricks. Hendron had no choice but to order his men to remove the walls and start again. At this point, the typically optimistic Hendron began showing signs of concern for the project as a whole, relaying to his colleagues in Santa Fe that, "We can keep trying, but how successful we will be is another story. The old house may be "jinxed," but my theory is that the constant rains did not give it a chance to dry."[16] By this point, the WPA and Museum of New Mexico had invested nearly $2,400.00 and three months of work into the project, and Hendron rallied his team the next week and began duplicating their efforts to save the east wall.

With a renewed sense of purpose, Hendron and the team restarted work on the east wall the week of July 23, 1938. The disastrous rain cleared up slightly, enough for them to move forward confidently. To better ensure success, Hendron elected to reinforce the foundation on which the adobes rested across the whole length of the wall. He instructed the crew to level the previously set foundation again and add concrete to the middle section of the wall where most of the weight from the roof would sit. The men removed all of the doors again, this time replacing their footings with limestone blocks set in cement and raising them above the level of the rest of the foundation. The first courses of the new wall appeared straighter than the first attempt, and Hendron felt confident that the effort would prove successful. Still worried about the wet weather, Hendron took a gamble aimed at keeping the adobe bricks dry. He ordered his men to move the bricks to the old second-floor courtroom space for storage. After relocating the adobes, he observed that "there are 58,000 lbs. of adobe blocks on the floor of the big room upstairs, so I think we need not worry about too many people being crowded in it."[17]

By mid-August, the elusive flue tiles finally arrived, and work on the east side chimneys began. Hendron seemed confident in his plan to tie the adobes from the chimney into the walls, distributing the weight more evenly. The original construction in 1873 consisted of a smaller fireplace set in each of the four rooms located on the east side of the building. This configuration did not place adverse strain on the wall, unlike the large central chimney that "was a bright idea of the county with forethought that it would weaken the main wall."[18] On August 20, 1938, Hendron and his team completed their second attempted restoration of the Courthouse's east wall. The final chimney configuration included three flues, two for the bottom-floor units and one for the second-floor fireplace. As workers installing the separate flues neared the roof line, they cut and laid the tiles so that the flues converged near the top—allowing masons to stack the final exterior chimney bricks in a manner replicating the former one. Hendron claimed a tempered victory over the challenging east wall and initially began planning to move on to other areas of the building. However, out of caution, he elected to leave the supports along the east wall to ensure the structure had time to settle under its weight before removing them and potentially disturbing other parts of the building. After a week of dry weather, workers removed the supports and gingerly lowered the roof onto the supporting wall. To Everyone's relief, the wall held with no noticeable bulges or issues. After careful measurement with transit, Hendron estimated that the wall had shifted less than one-eighth of an inch after removing the supports.[19] The only noticeable issue surfaced when the excess weight on the new upstairs chimney caused small cracks. To fix this, the crew simply removed adobes to the depth of the fissures and reset them over an artificial foundation—a remedy that, to this day, seems to have worked brilliantly. With many lessons learned, Hendron and his crew set their sights on their next tasks.

In September 1938, the crew turned their attention to the north, or front wall of the building. Settling of the wall had led to the entire facade sinking several inches. This movement caused the doors and windows along the north side of the building to fall out of line, warp, and even break under pressure in some cases. One significant cause for this drastic settling along the front of the building was the large balcony and double staircase. Although the balcony itself dated to the construction of the building in 1873, the county had added or improved on the additional heavy staircases in the 1881, 1890, and 1901. This extra weight added significant stress to the structure and contributed to water splashing

Lincoln County resident, Betty Seiler, visited the Courthouse construction site in 1939. The east wall scaffolding can be seen in the background and the retaining wall along the north side of the building constructed by Jerome Hendron's crew.
Lincoln County Historical Society

back onto the adobe and the window and doors under the balcony roof line. In the case of the large main entrance, Hendron's crew needed to rebuild part of the feature due to excessive wood rot. Based on experience along the east wall, the team reset the foundations under the door frames with lime blocks set in cement, and the entire new wall lifted nearly five feet above the foundation to guarantee adequate drainage.[20] Work on the rest of the building's exterior walls continued throughout September much faster than the work on the east wall had. Hendron and the crew encountered many of the same challenges experienced during their earlier efforts during the summer—applying their collectively gained knowledge of the building's distinctive architectural nature to overcome every obstacle placed before them. One unique challenge that the building presented was the general bulging of the wall across the entire second floor. Hendron noted that this issue primarily derived from how "unsatisfactory adobes are when they are laid higher than about ten or twelve feet."[21] To combat this pervasive issue, Hendron ran large metal rods fitted with plates through the attic space to square and secure the second-story walls. By October 1938, crews had finished all substantial structural work on the courthouse walls, and preparation began for stuccoing the entire exterior.[22]

While hindered by rain during the summer of 1938, Hendron's crew did not sit idly by, continuing work on the building's interior. This work included removing many partition walls the county and school board added between 1881 and the 1920s. Hendron noted in his report that previous laborers had constructed these interior walls from poorly made adobes and that the bricks crumbled when his team began demolishing them.[23] Due to the high costs of bricks, the crew cut new doorways into both vaults, using the salvaged bricks to finish building the new chimney above the roof line along the east wall. The new door leading into the vault, constructed by Littell in 1886, would also allow guests to view the inside of the structure without entering the Curator's office and living quarters planned for the rooms formerly occupied by the Post Office and L.G. Murphy's office.[24] On the second floor, the fireplaces in the courtroom were in such poor condition that workers completely reconstructed them, replacing the fireboxes and sanding and repainting the mantles white. To match the building's original flat white paint, Hendron drained the oil from his modern paint and thinned it with flattening oil. Finally, the laborers cut a new door from the main front room directly into the stairwell to the second floor—presenting visitors with a pathway upstairs without needing to go through the backrooms.

Once Hendron addressed the major stabilization issues and the interior renovations, his team began work on the 4,400-square-foot roof in October 1938. Hendron's goal regarding the roof was to copy the style of cedar shakes after the "oldest house I can find in Lincoln County," and return the roof line to its 1881 look.[25] The crew removed the ventilator added in 1886 that extended through the roof and topped with a cupola. The weight of this fixture had caused significant pressure on the roof rafters, causing them to sink several inches. The workers added a new central chimney along the western corner of George Peppin's 1903 vault, setting it on a nine-inch-thick concrete foundation and building the interior from the excess adobes made for the exterior walls. The flues extended into the front and rear rooms, and Hendron sourced old-style red bricks from Carrizozo to ensure the new chimney matched the remaining historic chimneys as closely as possible. Once they completed the new chimney and removed the cupola, the crew covered the roof with more resilient cedar shingles— an improvement over the original pine shingles cut at Paul Dowlin's Mill.[26] After two months of work, the team completed the work on the roof a week before Christmas 1938.[27]

During the colder months, Hendron focused on tasks his men could complete while working inside the building. By the end of October 1938, most of the glass for the building's windows had arrived, and installation began. The first windows to receive the new glass were along the reconstructed east side of the building. Hendron chose this room first because, with the newly built fireplace, the space offered a prime location to begin sanding and refinishing the remaining doors, mantle pieces, and other wooden features of the building.[28] Hendron also capitalized on the fortuitous arrival of a WPA truck for his use. In early November, Hendron hauled eighteen yards (over twenty tons) of quality quartz sand from the vicinity of the WPA "girl's camp" located at the old Baca sheep camp approximately twelve miles from Lincoln. In his estimation, the project needed thirty yards worth of sand to make enough plaster to cover both the interior and exterior of the building—in the end, the project required more than fifty yards.[29] Paying attention to details, Hendron intended to finish the interior walls of the building with traditionally fabricated *gaspe* plaster. *Gaspe* is historically made by dehydrating limestone, grinding it into a powder, burning it over an open fire, and re-hydrating it with water to the proper consistency. To this end, he set one of his workers to produce the material by hand. The unnamed craftsman crushed the limestone using a *mano* and *metate*, then burnt the *gaspe* over a large fire fueled by pinion juniper.[30]

This postcard image was taken during the last phases of Jerome Hendron's restoration work. Scaffolding is still present along the northwest wall and workers had not yet applied the final layer of plaster on the exterior of the building
Lincoln County Historical Society

By early December 1938, workers started plastering the interior walls of the building with a simple mud plaster as a base-coat and the handmade *gaspe* for the finish. Outside, laborers laid the foundation and walls for the vault toilet over a large pit dug the previous October. Work also commenced on the restoration of the front porch of the building under the supervision of a specialist carpenter hired by the WPA. The carpenter assisted Hendron in replacing the damaged pillars, repairing the balcony's flooring, and rebuilding the staircase on either side of the structure.[31] With 1938 coming to a close, the carpenters worked on completing the balcony, replacing all of the baseboards and wood trim throughout the building, repairing and refinishing the floors in the upstairs courtroom space, and plastering the interior walls.[32] While work was moving at a productive pace, Hendron was becoming increasingly pessimistic about seeing the project through to completion.

In January 1939, Hendron wrote to the Museum of New Mexico Assistant Director Dr. Reginald Fisher, explaining that he needed additional money and materials. Fisher recommended that Hendron try and complete the project using local funding, including money raised from the sale of the tin roofing removed from the building.[33] While Hendron labored to secure more money and resources, his team continued working, oblivious to the raging bureaucratic battle behind the scenes. The crew began plastering the interior of the building, starting on the final *gaspe* coat in late January 1939. On the outside of the building, carpenters finished work on the balcony and the custom-made cornices and wood trim.[34] By all outward appearances, the project was progressing well, but Hendron was in for yet another surprise

In addition to money woes, the WPA ordered Hendron to complete the project by April 5, 1939.[35] With time and money running short, Hendron convinced the Lincoln County Board of Education to fund, in part, the landscaping around the building. The additional landscaping included a wooden fence around the structure that Hendron and his crew designed based on the historic images they reviewed. At the same time, workers built the fence, Hendron finished the design and directed the team in the final construction of the simple outdoor restroom behind the Courthouse.[36] In the interest of time and funds, Hendron chose not to plant cottonwood trees along the east end of the building but rather substitute them with faster-growing Chinese Elm trees.

The last-minute landscaping projects represented the least of Hendron's concerns. With an impossible deadline of April 5th looming, the entire exterior of the Courthouse remained unplastered and unprotected. The delay in this critical project component was partly due to ongoing debates regarding what type and color of exterior covering should be applied. There were a small number of locals insistent on finishing the exterior walls with white plaster. To his credit, Hendron vehemently opposed this idea, stating in a letter to Assistant Director Fisher that:

> *In the event a white coat is put on the front of the building, the museum would receive a great deal of sarcastic criticism from a great many people who really know how the courthouse was in the beginning. It was just mud, and if the color is changed, it will not be a reconstruction and will depart from the entire scheme the museum has tried to put into effect.*[37]

Hendron received permission from the WPA to extend the project until May 20th to complete the plastering work, but additional money, materials, or laborers did not accompany the time extension.[38] Hendron considered leaving the adobes uncovered or simply plastering them with plain mud to save money and time.[39] The crew experimented with this simple solution on the detached restrooms and patches on the main structure. Although the method worked, Hendron was rightfully concerned that it would not last and that the museum would not have the resources to repair the exterior every year. With time running out, Hendron again turned to the local community for assistance, who gladly raised funds for more durable plaster. Hendron and his team covered the entire building exterior with a thick undercoat of traditional adobe mud plaster comprised of equal parts of locally sourced sand and dirt. This first layer cracked when dried, allowing adequate bonding with the two thinner one-eighth-inch top coats.[40] The final coats consisted of three parts of sand mixed with one part of dirt. To stabilize the mixture, Hendron added a commercial petroleum-based aggregate called bitmul—noting that the oil in the bitmul darkened the adobe plaster, enhancing the deep red color of the local dirt and leaving the final shade of the building a noticeably dark reddish brown. This darker color contrasted significantly with the stark white trim and new shutters installed on all six windows along the north side of the building—all of which were constructed by Museum of New Mexico staff in Santa Fe and shipped to Lincoln.[41]

There was also the issue of engineering proper drainage for the newly constructed roof. The freshly stabilized adobe walls were in danger of damage without a way to divert water from the building. Hendron was especially concerned about the front of the building, where he feared rain splashing back onto the walls from the exterior staircase could cause significant damage. Museum of New Mexico leadership shared Hendron's fears and agreed to pay for one hundred feet of gutters for the front of the structure. These gutters included downspouts at each corner, and workers painted the new elements white to match the building's cornices, windows, and doors.[42]

Hendron and his team completed their work on May 20, 1939, only nine hours before their deadline. In their final month of work, the WPA crew managed to plaster the entire exterior of the building, install gutters on the north-facing roof line, complete construction of the perimeter fence, and hang the custom-made shutters shipped from Santa Fe. Hendron opened his last letter from Lincoln to Assistant Director Fisher with the simple statement, "The Lincoln County Courthouse is now complete."[43] In his last official

Report to Dr. R. G. Fisher on the restoration of the old Lincoln County Court-house for the week ending May 20, 1939

There were only nine hours remaining in this work period. During that time the conductor pipes were all fastened to the eaves troughing and to the building and then painted white. The troughing received additional hangers. Rough places in the bituadobe plastering were smoothed over. The foundation was cleaned all around and the scaffolding torn down. The front yard and all of the grounds were raked clean.

The caretaker has begun the cleaning of all the woodwork which was left dirty due to plastering falling on it. He is now set up for housekeeping

We have completed the painting of the fence with one coat of white. It should have two but we have neither time or paint.

The caretaker has been instructed as to the high points of history concerning the building, the hours he is to work, how he is to keep his time, what he should do to keep the courthouse looking its best and something of the way to handle the visitors and to whom he should look for advice.

This completes the reconstruction of the Lincoln County Courthouse as far as time and money will permit. We did not have time to install the fixtures in the kitchen upstairs. This installation will cost only a few dollars however.

A set of completion pictures will follow this work report.

9 men employed during the week

```
          labor    Labor cost............. 32.72
    Add weekwill as of May 13, 1939......8007.43
          Total labor          $8040.15


    Sponsor's contribution:
          Material cost                    3.95
    To be paid by county (bitumuls)       35.70
                         Total            39.65

    Add material as of May 13,1939        1391.15
          Total material         $1430.80
    Travel exp. for may.                    2.50
                                        1433.30
    Total cost ..................    $9470.95
                                      9471.45
```

Signed: *J. W. Hendron*
J. W. Hendron, Supervisor,
Lincoln County Courthouse Project.

Jerome Hendron's final report to the Museum of New Mexico, May 20 1939
Lincoln County Historical Society

report, Hendron gave the total expenditures for the project $9,471.45—only $94.45 over the initially estimated budget submitted to the Works Progress Administration in December 1937.[44] With the physical work done, Hendron focused his attention on the orderly transfer of custodianship of the Courthouse Museum to the Museum of New Mexico. During the spring of 1939, Hendron lobbied for the museum to appoint a local to the permanent post of custodian. Hendron's preferred candidate for the position was twenty-eight-year-old Juan Bautista Zamora. Born and raised in Lincoln, Zamora worked for the WPA and labored alongside Hendron throughout the restoration project.[45] Fisher agreed to the recommendation, appointing Zamora to work alongside an interim local curator.[46] For that position, Fisher hired Mrs. Ruth Penfield, a longtime Lincoln resident who, along with her husband John, operated the mercantile formerly owned by John Tunstall and James Dolan.[47]

Soon after Hendron's departure, state and local officials began planning for a grand opening and dedication of the new museum. State Senator Perry Sears and his wife Helen chaired the local planning committee, working to ensure that as many dignitaries as possible could attend.[48] Senator Sears also worked with the Museum of New Mexico to relocate some artifacts and artwork for the new museum so that the walls would not be embarrassingly bare during the ceremony. These temporary exhibits included an exhibition of artwork created by Fort Stanton Hospital Administrator Dan Kusiniovich—most recently on display at the Museum of Art in Santa Fe.

On Sunday, July 30, 1939, more than 1,500 people gathered along the street in front of the courthouse in Lincoln to participate in the new museum's official dedication. Dignitaries traveled from every corner of the state to attend the affair, including Governor John E. Miles. Miles later noted in an interview that the ceremony was unique because three former Governors—George Curry, Miguel Otero Jr., and James Hinkle—also attended.[49] Assistant Director Reginald Fisher served as the master of ceremonies for the dedication. WPA representative Isabel Lancaster Eckles presented on her organization's behalf, detailing the work completed by Hendron and his team, the LCSAHA, and the Museum of New Mexico. In a brief lecture, Hendron spoke about his team's efforts after former Regulator George Coe provided his recollections entitled "Reminiscences of Old Lincoln County." New Mexico State Senator for Lincoln and Otero Counties, Perry Sears accepted the WPA's presentation on behalf of the local and state delegations.

Following the official ceremony at the courthouse in Lincoln, attendees traveled to the Capitan Union High School, where the Capitan Women's Club sponsored a banquet. Following the meal, Museum of New Mexico Supervisor of Branch Museums Albert G. Ely outlined plans for exhibits in the new museum. Senator Louise Coe delivered a speech entitled, "What the Old Courthouse Museum will mean to Lincoln County."[50] Unfortunately, a record of Senator Coe's talk has not survived, but the new museum's impact on Lincoln would be longstanding and significant. The dedication of the Courthouse Museum and Lincoln Monument established the foundation for additional restoration work in

Program for the Celebration Banquet for the Courthouse Museum opening, held on July 30, 1939
Lincoln County Historical Society

Governor John E. Miles speaking at the dedication of the Courthouse Museum on July 30, 1939
Lincoln County Historical Society

The fully restored Lincoln County Courthouse as it looked in the summer of 1939
Lincoln County Historical Society

CHAPTER TWELVE
THE MUSEUM YEARS

John Sinclair during a radio broadcast from the Courthouse Museum, 1941
Lincoln County Historical Society

Following the opening of the Courthouse Museum in July 1939, Juan Zamora and Ruth Penfield maintained the building and opened the doors each morning for visitors. Very few artifacts adorned the newly opened museum, aside from a few sparsely filled exhibit cases located in the two largest rooms on the first floor, dubbed the "Hall of Archaeology" and the "Hall of History."[1] The Museum of New Mexico needed a full-time curator to assist them in installing new exhibits. They found a willing candidate when they appointed author and historian John Leslie Sinclair to the position in May 1940. The museum offered Sinclair sixty dollars per month and allowed him to live in the former county clerk's office on the eastern end of the first floor.[2] Sinclair's background made him uniquely qualified for the position in Lincoln. Sinclair was born in New York City in 1902 to John Sinclair and Gertrude Corbin. The elder John Sinclair belonged to a wealthy and aristocratic family from Northern Scotland, but his wife Gertrude came from a poor Irish family living in New York. Sinclair's Scottish family never accepted Gertrude into the family, and when his father died in 1912, they sent ten-year-old John to live with his grandfather and uncle in Britain.

In 1923, John Sinclair returned to America to help establish a ranch for his family in British Columbia. However, upon stepping off a train in New Mexico, Sinclair immediately decided that the American Southwest was where he belonged. Disinherited by his family, Sinclair spent fourteen years working as a cowboy,

John Sinclair's dog inside the gated yard of the Courthouse Museum, 1941.
Lincoln County Historical Society

including in Lincoln County, before moving to Santa Fe to pursue a career in writing. In 1936, the Museum of New Mexico employed Sinclair to write articles regarding upcoming exhibits at the Palace of the Governors. Then, in 1940, the museum hired him as the Courthouse Museum's first full-time curator.[3] When Sinclair took over operations at the Courthouse, he described the building as "...absolutely empty. There was nothing in there except for white walls, and everything was fresh and clean."[4]

Sinclair set up his office and living quarters in the rooms on the eastern side of the first floor, with a small kitchen in the rear storeroom area. Hendron's work did not include the addition of interior plumbing, so Sinclair retrieved water from a cistern across the street at Roman Maes' *La Paloma Bar*. Sinclair assisted in setting up display cases

The second floor "Indian Room" after installation of cases and artifacts
Lincoln County Historical Society

shipped by truck from Santa Fe, filling them with artifacts requisitioned from the museum's permanent exhibitions. These artifacts included religious art comprised of *Santos* and depictions of the *Stations of the Cross*; various Southwestern indigenous pottery; a small collection of Kachina dolls; and a few items related to the Mescalero Apache culture.[5] Sinclair organized these items within the former billiard room on the first floor, christening it the "Indian Room." Sinclair dedicated the main first-floor room to artifacts related to the "frontier times" in Lincoln, including handmade dioramas depicting episodes from the region's past, including Billy the Kid's famous escape from the building in 1881.

To finish filling out the empty cases, Sinclair worked with local citizens, including Edward Penfield, who provided dozens of artifacts from his private collection. According to Sinclair, not all community members were excited about his appointment. Despite his years of working and living in Lincoln County, some citizens believed that the best person for the job of curator at the Lincoln Museum was a native of Lincoln itself. Sinclair did not necessarily disagree, repeatedly turning to locals for help while in charge. Sinclair's efforts proved successful, with over ten thousand guests visiting the Courthouse in 1941, including nearly three thousand during the busiest month of the year, August.[6]

Living in the cavernous building alone certainly affected Sinclair, and in his memoirs, he described living in the building in this way:

One of the original dioramas displayed in the Courthouse Museum, depicting Billy the Kid's escape from the building in 1881
Lincoln County Historical Society

There was a strange feeling in the courthouse. It was spooky as could be! You felt creatures around you…you felt it in the air. I lived in the courthouse and right under where Billy the Kid shot Olinger. There was an upper balcony outside and steps going up on either side of the building. Sometimes, in the middle of the night, I'd hear sounds from up above, from the end of the balcony. The only lighting I had was a Coleman lamp and a stable lamp. So I would pick up the stable lamp and start upstairs. I climbed those stairs where Billy shot his guard, Bell, and you could sometimes feel him when going up those steps…you had better step over the bodies! I would go up there, and, of course, there was nothing there. But all the same, you had to watch in case someone climbed up onto the balcony trying to get in.[7]

John Sinclair arrived in Lincoln at a fascinating time. Not only had the state recently opened the Courthouse Museum, but community members were planning and preparing for a unique event that would ultimately become a significant driver of tourism for the town. In 1934, state and local leaders in New Mexico began discussing commemorating the four-hundredth anniversary of the European settlement of New Mexico by Francisco Coronado. In 1935, the state legislature created the New Mexico Coronado Cuarto Centennial Commission and tasked the group with planning a year-long celebration in 1940. That same year, New Mexico politician Clinton Anderson secured $200,000.00 in federal funding to support the festival, which included partnerships with Texas, Arizona, Mexico, and Spain. Headed by the University of New Mexico President J.F. Zimmerman, the Coronado Commission solicited ideas from communities across the state to fulfill Governor Clyde Tingley's desire to host more than a dozen historic pageants as part of the celebration.

The residents of Lincoln County, led by Senator Louise Coe and artist Peter Hurd, brought an exciting proposal to the table.[8] The community members suggested performing an outdoor folk pageant, retelling the story of Billy the Kid, on the grounds of the Historic Courthouse in Lincoln. As Artistic Director and star, Hurd wrote the script for the play based on previous work by Santa Fe novelist and playwright Phillip Stevenson. In 1931, Stevenson wrote the playscript for an outdoor folk pageant called *Sure Fire: Episodes in the Life of Billy the Kid*, performed for the first time during the annual Santa Fe Fiesta.[9] Hurd adapted Stevenson's play, renaming it *Billy the Kid Lives Again*—although many

Artist Peter Hurd portrays Billy the Kid during the first performance of *Billy the Kid Rides Again.* The performance occurred on the lawn behind the Courthouse Museum and used the building as a backdrop
Lincoln County Historical Society

Costumed Fiesta Dancers during Lincoln's Coronado Cuarto Centennial Celebration
Lincoln County Historical Society

newspapers still referred to it as *Sure Fire*. Organizers set the performance date for June 22, 1940, and surrounded the debut with additional events. Coined "Three Days in Old Lincoln," the festivities started on Thursday, June 20th, 1940, with the traditional wedding of San Patricio residents Leo Pena and Mary Gonzalez held at the *La Iglesia de San Juan Bautista* in Lincoln. That afternoon, Elizabeth Garrett—daughter of former Lincoln County Sheriff Patrick Garrett—performed her song "O Fair New Mexico," adopted in 1917 as the official state song of New Mexico.

Following Garrett's performance, a series of dignitaries delivered speeches, including former Governors John Miles and F.J. Hinkle, as well as the University of New Mexico President J.F. Zimmerman. The evening concluded with the first-ever performance of *Billy the Kid Lives Again*, with Peter Hurd playing the title character, supported by a cast of over one hundred and fifty community members.[10]

During John Sinclair's tenure, the author and historian greeted visitors to the Courthouse Museum, researched the region's history, and designed and built new exhibits. The Museum of New Mexico installed several traveling exhibits during the early years of the museum's operation, and visitation steadily increased. This growth in funding and visitation sharply decreased when the United States entered World War II, and federal and state officials began diverting more public funds toward the war effort. Sinclair's time in Lincoln was not only spent working to enhance the museum itself. Sinclair continued working on his first book, The Bean Harvest. The book drew inspiration from Sinclair's life and experiences in Southern New Mexico, following the story of a homesteading family in the Estancia Valley. Sinclair completed the manuscript while working and living in Lincoln, submitting the finished product to Scottish publishing company *Macmillan* in 1942.

Shortly after submitting his book for review, John Sinclair resigned from his position in Lincoln on November 15, 1942, and moved to Tucson to focus on his writing career.[11] Sinclair indicated in later correspondence that he based his decision to depart, at least partially, on the possible appointment of former Governor George Curry as State Historian and his divorce from his wife Ruth after only two months of marriage.[12] Although this would not occur until 1945, conversations among state and museum officials happened as early as 1942. While in Tucson the following year, Sinclair received word that Macmillan had accepted his book for publishing, although with a suggested name change. Published as In Time of Harvest, the book was a commercial and critical success for Sinclair and is considered one of New Mexico's most significant literary contributions of the 20th century.[13] Sinclair's time in Tucson was short-lived, and he moved back to New Mexico in the mid-1940s. The author returned to public service in 1949, managing the Coronado Historic Site for the Museum of New Mexico, where he served until his retirement in the mid-1960s.

Sinclair's departure surprised the Museum of New Mexico and left them without an immediate replacement. Between November 1942 and November 1943, Mrs. Clara O'Bryant served as temporary caretaker for the museum earning $10.00 per month and living in the room formally occupied by John Sinclair.[14] Following Clara O'Bryant's resignation, the Museum of New Mexico appointed Theodora Maes, wife of Roman Maes, to serve as the caretaker at the Courthouse. Mrs. Maes served in this position until 1947, while the Museum of New Mexico searched for a permanent curator with the experience needed to expand the facility's operation.[15]

On April 11, 1945, Governor John Dempsey signed Senate Bill 158, formally establishing the appointed position of State Historian of New Mexico. Governor Dempsey quickly named former Territorial Governor and Lincoln County resident George Curry to the post, and Curry began his largely symbolic duties as the state's authority on the past.[16]

**Curator and former Territorial Governor George Curry (center) during
his open house held at the Courthouse Museum in August 1947**
Lincoln County Historical Society

In a letter thanking Dempsey, Curry outlined his simple goals as State Historian, "...to devote the remainder of the time that I have to perpetuate the memory of the good men and women who have done so much to build up our wonderful state."[17]

In 1947, Curry accepted reappointment as State Historian, with the caveat that he be allowed to move to Lincoln and reside in the curator's residence. The Museum of New Mexico agreed to the plan, and new legislation for the position included the stipulation that the State Historian's "...residence shall be in the Courthouse Museum in Lincoln.[18] Curry took on the additional title of the Old Courthouse Museum custodian and moved into the building in May 1947.[19] Within days of taking over duties from Theodora Maes, Curry began working on updating exhibits in the Courthouse, primarily with items from his private collection.

In June 1947, the New Mexico State Finance Board authorized an advance of $3,000.00 on Curry's annual salary so that he might work on redecorating and improving the galleries at the Courthouse Museum.[20] Beyond improvements to the building itself, Curry also used his time in Lincoln to reconnect with old friends and colleagues and to organize his archives and documents, chronicling his colorful life. In August 1947, Curry hosted a reception at the Courthouse Museum celebrating the fiftieth anniversary of his leaving Lincoln County in 1897. Curry invited "all old-time residents of Lincoln County" and sitting Governor Thomas Mabry, former Governors John Miles and J.F. Hinkle, and Brigadier General Hugh M. Milton II—recently appointed as President of New Mexico State University.[21] Curry fell ill shortly after this gala affair and died on November 27, 1947, at the Albuquerque Veterans Hospital.[22]

Since John Sinclair's departure in 1942, the Courthouse Museum in Lincoln had operated under the direction of untrained caretakers and a small staff of docents. Following George Curry's death, the Museum of New Mexico elected to reevaluate the situation in Lincoln, employing journalist William Robinson of the "Roswell Morning Dispatch" and history professor Colonel Maurice G. Fulton from the New Mexico Military Institute to analyze operations at the Courthouse Museum. Fulton and Robinson's evaluation and recommendations galvanized the Museum of New Mexico to act, and in early 1948, the museum offered Colonel Fulton an unpaid position as an advisor. The situation at the Courthouse worsened when caretaker Jessie Gallagher became ill and could not keep up with his duties. In June 1948, Colonel Fulton resigned from the New Mexico Military Institute, accepted a full-time position as superintendent of Lincoln State Monument, and moved into the living quarters on the museum's first floor. When Fulton took over in Lincoln, the Museum of New Mexico's budget was in dire straits, and a decade of deferred maintenance on the restored Courthouse was beginning to take its toll. Administration officials recommended that Fulton explore reviving the local historical society in Lincoln to try and raise funds for maintaining the large building and enhancing exhibits. Fulton struggled to balance work on his personal writing

Colonel Maurice G. Fulton outside of a home in Lincoln, NM, c. 1930
Lincoln County Historical Society

projects with the consuming tasks associated with simply keeping the doors open at the museum. He almost immediately began providing grim updates to his superiors regarding the status of operations in Lincoln. In a letter to Museum of New Mexico Research Associate Edwin Ferndon in February 1949, Colonel Fulton described the situation in Lincoln in these colorful terms:

> *The attendance report is so sleazy that I have not hastened to submit it. The total is a beggerly 60. Incident to the cold weather, traffic was very light. As you know, the building is far from weatherproof. Doors with cracks large enough to admit even snow; windows decidedly leaky around the window frames. Throughout January, the building absorbed cold in the succession of days with temperatures remaining below freezing, with wind adding to the uncomfortableness. Result, I hung out a sign that the building was too uncomfortable and that visiting it was the peril of health.[23]*

Local frustration with the Museum of New Mexico's operation in Lincoln encouraged community members to explore establishing an independent commission to run the branch museum. In 1949, the state legislature approved Senate Bill 213, creating the Old Lincoln County Memorial Commission. Signed into law by Governor Thomas Mabry, the Commission's mandate was simple—to supervise operations at the Old Lincoln County Courthouse Museum. The Commission consisted of nine members, one appointed by the governor from each of the counties formerly part of Lincoln County and one from the state at large.[24] Beyond the Commission's creation, the authorizing legislation also appropriated a modest annual budget of $10,000.00 to maintain and run the museum.[25] The first nine members of the Commission included longtime Lincoln resident Burt

Members of the Old Lincoln County Memorial Commission, 1956.
Lincoln County Historical Society

139

Pfingsten and Lea County resident Dessie Sawyer—mother of pioneering female rodeo star Fern Sawyer.[26] The commission elected Dessie Sawyer, who also served as the Chairwoman of the New Mexico Democratic Party, as its first chairwoman. Sawyer, Pfingsten, and the rest of the commission saw great potential for the Courthouse Museum and Lincoln as significant contributors to the region's tourism economy.

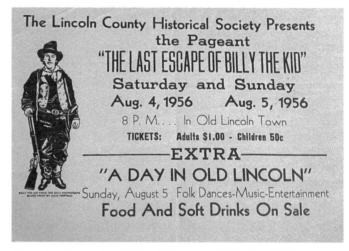

Flyer for the revived "Last Escape of Billy the Kid" pageant, 1956.
Lincoln County Historical Society

One of the commission's first significant projects was the resurrection of the "Day in Old Lincoln" festival and the Billy the Kid folk pageant. In 1949, the commission partnered with the Lincoln County Historical Society to hold the *Last Escape of Billy the Kid* pageant and festival for the first time since 1940. The Old Lincoln County Memorial Commission provided space for the outdoor performance on the grounds of the Courthouse Museum and organized additional events around town. Peter Hurd reprised his role as Billy the Kid in the play, now called *The Last Escape of Billy the Kid.*[27] The Old Lincoln County Memorial Commission utilized the event as a fundraiser for the Courthouse Museum and other projects, and their vision paid off. The resurrection of the event became an annual occurrence, contributing significantly to public support for preserving Lincoln and enhancing the museum at the Courthouse.

By 1950, the Memorial Commission issued its first report on its activities, further defining its objective to "preserve and restore the original buildings and their grounds in this historic spot" and to "provide adequate explanation and interpretation of this significance." During their first year in control of the Courthouse Museum, the commission defined and verified the legal boundaries of the property while completing much-needed repairs on the building. Beyond physical improvements, the commission also added a new exhibit displaying photographs and documents collected by former Governor George

of county affairs demanded a larger building; the spacious and multi-room stone building supplanted the three-room adobe that had done duty as a county building for ten years.

For thirty-three years the building continued service as headquarters for administrative and judicial matters. Then with the change of county seat to Carrizozo, it was given to the County School Board as an addition to the Lincoln Public School. Classes were held in it sporadically whenever the regular school building proved inadequate. In spite of being still in use, the building suffered so much neglect that it was on the verge of being declared unsafe and demolished. Its friends, however, rallied to its help, and in 1937 secured legislation that made it the ward of the State in charge of the Museum of New Mexico. With the oncoming of the World War, the Museum was forced to curtail its activities, but in 1947, Ex-Governor George Curry, State Historian, secured approval to his having office and residence in the building, with complete control. Upon his death in late 1947, the Museum of New Mexico again assumed charge. Many persons, however, believed that its development as a regional museum would be advanced by having an autonomous board in charge. Accordingly the legislature of 1949 created the Old Lincoln County Memorial Commission, which is responsible for the maintenance and operation of the building.

The Commission decided that this landmark should be treated as an historic house type of museum. The Commission has therefore tried to subscribe to accepted principles for managing this kind of historic shrine. First among these is preserving and protecting as much as possible of the original building and surrounding grounds. Second comes keeping before the public the part it has played in the life of southeast New Mexico. This explanatory and interpretive duty involves ade-

quate attendants as well as pertinent displays of maps, documents, contemporary photographs, books by local authors, and the like. The Commission, therefore, collects, consolidates, and disseminates at the Old Courthouse, reliable information concerning the history, legends, and traditions of southeast New Mexico. In the George Curry collection of photographs of eminent New Mexicans, it has the start of obtaining the names and personal appearance of the earliest settlers of this area.

The Commission believes that the restorations described in this leaflet, and any others that may fall under its care, offer large possibilities for recreation, education, and inspiration for all classes of people. It pledges itself to restore accurately and to preserve enduringly historic sites and buildings especially those belonging to the formative periods of this section of New Mexico.

NEW MEXICO COUNTIES IN 1880
After Coan's History of New Mexico

Torreon Watch-Tower and Refuge

THE COMMISSION

Appointed by Governor Thomas J. Mabry from recommendations by County Commissioners of eight counties concerned.

HAROLD R. MILLER, Chairman
Carlsbad, Eddy County
BERT PFINGSTEN, Vice-Chairman
Lincoln, Lincoln County
JIM COOLEY, Secretary-Treasurer
Roswell, Chaves County
MRS. U. D. SAWYER
Crossroads, Lea County
MRS. ORA LEE SKIPWORTH
Fort Sumner, DeBaca County
G. W. CARR
Portales, Roosevelt County
ALFRED HUNTER
Alamogordo, Otero County
W. H. DUCKWORTH
Clovis, Curry County
E. G. HAWKINS
Farmington, State-at-Large

DESIGNED BY CARL HERTZOG

Restorations
IN
HISTORIC
LINCOLN
NEW MEXICO

*Official Leaflet issued by
Old Lincoln County Memorial Commission
1950*

Lincoln County Memorial Commission Guide to Lincoln, 1950
Lincoln County Historical Society

LINCOLN, NEW MEXICO

LINCOLN started in the 1850s when a cluster of Spanish-American families moved from the vicinity of Socorro in the Rio Grande Valley and planted themselves in the valley of the Bonito. They displayed the hardihood of frontiersmen in adventuring into a section belonging to Apaches. In naming the town they delighted to honor the watercourse, so all important to their welfare, and called the place La Placita del Rio Bonito.

The settlement had no historian, but the scanty early records reveal familiar Spanish surnames, such as Chaves, Gomez, Gonzales, Miranda, Montano, Salazar, Trujillo. These people lived the pastoral life of the Spanish people, deriving an unpretentious living from their small farms and herds. A limited number of the more enterprising engaged in freighting or storekeeping. The Civil War came and went, leaving the village undis-

turbed, but a new epoch began immediately afterward. Rebuilding Fort Stanton brought a change in the economy of the people of La Placita. At the Fort they found a market for their produce as well as employment as laborers or craftsmen. The number of adobe houses increased to forty or fifty. Discharged soldiers liked the Valley and became residents. Other enterprising spirits came to advantage themselves by the opportunities for making fortunes rapidly in a new country.

With the formation of Lincoln County in 1869 out of the eastern area of Socorro County, La Placita attained the rank of county-seat. The Anglo element naturally became more pronounced and even more dominant. The Spanish element remained docile, industrious, and law-abiding, but with the Anglos, most of whom were more sojourners, came turmoil and disorder which put the County into ill-repute.

Photograph courtesy of Mrs. Henry Fritz, Capitan, New Mexico

TORREON

IN THE CENTER of the town stands a round structure of stone representative of the beginnings of Lincoln. This Torreon was the fortification the early Spanish-American settlers built for the double purpose of a watch-tower and a refuge from marauding Indians. The two rooms some fifteen feet in diameter and barely eight feet high, would hold the women and children, while several of the men might crouch behind the four foot parapet.

Most of the time a guard was stationed on top who scanned the Valley for signs of Indians. If any were noted, he hastened down crude ladders until he reached the lowest room, mounted the horse kept there, and rode out to give the alarm up and down the Valley. The populace rushed to the Torreon and remained within its thick walls until the danger passed. In later times, when dangers of new character appeared, the structure continued useful. During the Harrell War of 1873, it was a

refuge for women and children from the dreaded Tejanos. Again in 1878 during the Lincoln County War Murphy forces used it, not so much defensively, but aggressively against the McSween group.

As the years passed, disuse and neglect took their toll and reduced the Torreon almost to ruins. Its friends in Lincoln and elsewhere united themselves to accomplish its restoration. The Southern Pacific deeded the property to the State, and the Chaves County Historical Society raised the necessary funds for a W P A project. The restoration started and by February 1935 the tower was ready for dedication as a monument to a turning-point in the development of southeastern New Mexico.

Old Lincoln County Courthouse

THE WESTERN edge of Lincoln displays a building of even greater importance than the Torreon. In its life of more than seventy-five years, the building has played several parts. First the large mercantile establishment of L. G. Murphy & Co., doing a large business throughout the County in the latter 1870s. In 1877, powerful competition developed. The new store founded by John H. Tunstall, advanced rapidly in the esteem and patronage of the citizens. Both stores became victims of the Lincoln County War. In 1880 the County bought the Murphy building with considerable of its adjoining land. Efficient administration

Lincoln County Memorial Commission Guide to Lincoln, 1950
Lincoln County Historical Society

Curry.[28] Further defining the Old Lincoln County Memorial Commission's role at the Courthouse Museum, the state legislature passed SB213 during their 1951 session. This bill prohibited the Museum of New Mexico from making any changes in the "Old Lincoln County Courthouse" without consent from the Old Lincoln County Commission. Although the museum still owned the physical property, this new statute gave the commission and the curators they hired complete operational control of the building.[29] In 1951, Governor Edward Mechem appointed lawyer, author, and historian William A. Keleher to the commission. Keleher was a close friend of the late George Curry and an avid researcher and author of New Mexico history. Over the next twenty years, Keleher would be instrumental in guiding the direction of the Old Lincoln County Memorial Commission and its expanding efforts to preserve historic Lincoln beyond just the Courthouse Museum.[30]

Unfortunately, curator Fulton's enthusiasm and energy did not match that of the commission members. The group needed a leader to help take operations in Lincoln to a new level. However, Fulton seemed more interested in finishing his book on the Lincoln County War than attending to the daily needs of the museum. Increasingly frustrated with his duties interfering with his research and writing, Fulton resigned from his position and returned to Roswell in September 1950.[31] Once again, needing a new leader for the Courthouse Museum, the Old Lincoln County Commission searched for the right person to replace Fulton. They did not have to look far, as a qualified, motivated, and energetic candidate arrived in town that summer to take over as director of the *Last Escape of Billy the Kid* pageant.

For the 1950 performance of *The Last Escape of Billy the Kid*, the memorial commission hired author and librarian Caroline Davis to direct the performance. Davis' husband, John, took over the role of Billy the Kid from Peter Hurd, and Caroline edited the script to be more historically accurate than Phillip Stevenson's original work. As they had in 1940 and 1949, community members performed the pageant on the grounds of the Old Courthouse, using the south-facing wall as the backdrop for the outdoor stage. Davis' successful work as Director of the pageant led to commission members offering her the position of curator-custodian at the Courthouse Museum. Davis accepted the job and began her tenure in Lincoln in December 1950.[32.]

Caroline and her husband, John Carter Davis, moved to Lincoln County to start a ranch after the end of World War II.[33] Caroline and John were born in Oklahoma, but John grew up on his grandfather's ranch in Kenna, New Mexico. John attended Oklahoma

A&M—now Oklahoma State University—and joined the U.S. Army Air Corps during the war.[34] Caroline attended the University of Oklahoma, where she studied library science. The young couple lived in the Courthouse's living quarters with their young children, Julie and Chris. Upon arrival, the motivated Davis immediately began improving both the exhibits and the physical state of the building.[35] Caroline utilized her library science degree, writing new interpretive panels, producing special events, and bringing in new exhibits. John Davis assisted Caroline with her work by constructing cases and other exhibit furniture for new displays and helping with general building maintenance.

Mrs. Caroline Davis Named Old Lincoln Court Custodian

Alfred Hunter, Otero county representative on the Lincoln County Memorial committee, attended the September 6 meeting of the group at Roswell at which Mrs. Caroline Davis of Hondo was named custodian of the old Lincoln courthouse. Mrs. Davis, author and director of the 1950 Day in Oold Lincoln pageant, will succeed Colonel Fulton whose resignation was effective September 1.

It was also decided at this special meeting that the colonel be permitted to continue with the research work he had already begun.

Announcement of Caroline Davis' appointed as Courthouse Custodian
Alamogordo Daily News
Alamogordo, New Mexico, Thursday, September 14, 1950

One of Caroline's many projects included the installations of temporary art exhibits displaying paintings and drawings by well-known western artist Mark Storm and local artist Dan Kusianovich. Storm was part owner of the 5-S ranch in the Ruidoso Valley but lived most of his time in Houston. His brother Dan Storm, an author and rancher, was a significant contributor to the annual *Last Escape of Billy the Kid* pageant and a strong supporter of Lincoln's preservation. A native of Croatia, Dan Kusianovich arrived in Lincoln County in 1923 as a patient and staff member at the Fort Stanton Public Health Service Hospital. He eventually worked his way up the ranks of the hospital staff to serve as the facility's Chief Clerk. While at Fort Stanton, Kusianovich perfected his artistic abilities, including sketches of noted Mescalero tribal members displayed in the Courthouse Museum collection.

The Davis' also spent their time as curators of the Courthouse Museum working on maintenance issues with the building. Although only a decade had passed since Jerome Hendron's building restoration, the structure was already suffering from neglect. These improvements included repairs to the old vault, replacement of the roof's wood shingles with fire-resistant asphalt shingles, and plaster repairs on both the inside and outside of the building.[36] To fund these projects, the commission successfully lobbied for increases in the annual operating budget for the museum, raising the yearly appropriation from $264.00 to $1,680 between 1949 and 1951—an increase of more than five hundred percent. Reports from the staff during the first years after the Old Lincoln County Memorial Commission took over the operation of the museum reinforce many of the challenges that still, to this day, affect operations in Lincoln. The rural location of Lincoln made it difficult for Caroline Davis and her staff to contract for work on the building, order and receive goods, and even keep the building heated at times. Despite these challenges, commission members described the staff during this time as follows:

> *...close-knit, harmonious group possessing a high degree of versatility—each one being proficient with the guest book, the broom, historical information, the wood pile, the rake, and hospitality, as each challenging situation requires.*[37]

(L to R) Nan Boylan, Johnny Miegs, and Si Salas, in the Curator's residence located in the Courthouse Museum, c. 1955
Lincoln County Historical Society

Caroline Davis' time as curator lasted only two years. In July 1952, Caroline, John, and their family relocated to Albuquerque, where John began a new career as a tractor salesman.[38] Before leaving, however, Caroline helped map out several vital enhancements to the building that would be carried to fruition by her replacement. These included the restoration of the old courtroom on the second floor, electrical updates aimed at enhancing exhibit capabilities, and plans for securing the old vault as storage for historical documents transferred from the County Courthouse in Carrizozo.

It did not take long for the Old Lincoln County Memorial Commission to find a suitable replacement for Caroline Davis. This time, their choice would remain in Lincoln for more than a decade and assisted them in significantly expanding their effort to preserve the town beyond the Courthouse Museum. In August 1952, the commission named John Lewis Boylan as the new curator of the Courthouse Museum. A native of Ohio, Boylan served as a medic during World War II, relocating to New Mexico with his wife, Nan, in 1947. John and Nan Boylan attended the University of New Mexico, where John graduated with a fine arts degree in 1948. In 1951, John accepted the position as Acting Director of the Roswell Museum of Art and History, dedicating himself to learning as much about the region's people and culture as possible.[39]

The exhibit dedicated to Governor McDonald included several of his wife, Francis', dresses worn at official functions
Lincoln County Historical Society

Like their predecessors, John and Nan Boylan worked as a team in Lincoln. During their first year at the Courthouse, the Boylans spearheaded several significant exhibit projects. In the old billiard hall, John Boylan installed an exhibit displaying additional Native American artifacts from the region—enhancing the existing "Indian Room," created by John Sinclair. The expanded exhibition included artifacts donated by community members, including Peter Hurd, Clark Pfingsten, and Mary Coe. John Boylan employed his fine art skills and added to the exhibit a series of hand-drawn maps and diagrams showing the location of archaeological excavations from the area and descriptions of the artifacts.[40]

The Boylans also expanded on the exhibit created by Caroline Davis, displaying artifacts belonging to

The Courthouse after the 1955 renovations and removal of the exterior staircases, c.1955
Lincoln County Historical Society

George Curry. At the time of his death in 1947, Curry was organizing his private papers and photograph collection, and the Davis' and Boylans' finished this lofty endeavor, creating space in the museum for their display. The new exhibition, called the "Governor's Corner," included additional artifacts belonging to the first governor of the State of New Mexico, William C. McDonald. McDonald began his career in public service in Lincoln County—serving as County Assessor, Chairman of the Lincoln County Commission, and Lincoln's representative to the state legislature.

The Boylan's final project during their first year as curators was a large-scale exhibit about the community of White Oaks and mining activities in the region. This exhibit took up most of the main room on the first floor and included photographs, old newspapers, mining records, and court documents stored in the old vault. Again, John Boylan created custom maps depicting regional mines, mail routes, and more. This exhibit opened on October 26, 1952, and former White Oaks residents from as far away as Silver City and Clovis traveled to attend the dedication. The Boylans and the commission continued working on the Courthouse building's physical upkeep, undertaking several maintenance and improvement projects between 1953 and 1956. Most notable was the removal of the exterior staircase, which occurred sometime between 1954 and 1956. This decision brought the building closer to what it looked like at the time of Billy the Kid's escape in

The Courthouse safe in Carrizozo shortly before being moved back to Lincoln
Lincoln County Historical Society

1881. The commission also worked on the Courthouse grounds, adding gravel to the pathways surrounding the structure and a sprinkler system for irrigating the lawn and trees.[41]

Following the success of these new exhibits, the Boylans and the Old Lincoln County Memorial Commission set their sights on an even larger project—the restoration and reconstruction of the second-floor courtroom and reinstallation of the original 1,200-pound *Diebold Safe and Lock Company* vault door. John Boylan spent two years researching the courtroom—conducting dozens of oral histories with locals who remembered details about the room. Boylan had to rely on these recollections because there were no existing images or drawings of the space during its time as a courtroom.[42] The Boylans reconstructed the jury box, railing, judge's dais, and gallery benches using these recollections.[43]

On June 20, 1954, nearly two hundred people crammed into the courtroom during the dedication ceremony for the new exhibit. Numerous dignitaries attended the event and listened to the speeches from their seats in the reconstructed jury box. Those in attendance included Governor Edwin Mechem, former New Mexico Attorney General Ott Askren, and former U.S. Deputy Marshal Dee Harkey. Presiding over the affair was 84-year-old Charles Brice, former Chief Justice of the New Mexico Supreme Court.[44] While restoring the courtroom, Boylan and the commission convinced the county of Lincoln to

The restored courtroom, c.1955
Lincoln County Historical Society

The Lincoln County Memorial Commission received an "Award of Merit" from the American Association of State and Local History for their restoration of the Lincoln Courthouse Courtroom, *Lincoln County Historical Society*

return the original vault door to the Courthouse. The Boylans resided in the curator's residence on the first floor of the building, so placing the door in its original location was not feasible. To compromise, workers added the door to the opening created by Jerome Hendron, which opened into the main entrance area. Although not historically accurate, this orientation allowed visitors to view the door without entering the Boylans' private living space.

The work of the Lincoln County Memorial Commission and the Boylans paid off significantly, as visitation to Lincoln and the Courthouse Museum continued to increase during the second half of the 1950s. In 1955, John Boylan reported that more than four thousand visitors came through the museum door in July alone. During the year, over twenty-four thousand tourists went through the museum, an increase of almost twenty-five percent over the previous year.[45] The steady increase in visitors forced the staff to abandon using a written register for guests and instead purchase a mechanical counter to keep track of visitation numbers.[46] Those interested in touring the museum paid one quarter for admission, collected by the museum's Assistant Curator and receptionist, long-time Lincoln resident Annie Ramey.[47]

With new exhibits in the Courthouse Museum and visitation in Lincoln at an all-time high, the Commission began to look beyond just the Courthouse and towards additional preservation opportunities in Lincoln. In 1955, John Boylan designed a new visitor guide for Lincoln, which he and his staff handed out at the Courthouse. The guide included historical information about the Courthouse and the town of Lincoln, Fort Stanton, White Oaks, and Billy the Kid. The booklet also contained a map created by John Boylan describing the historic structures throughout the entire town of Lincoln.[48] Fulfilling its mission to expand its preservation efforts in Lincoln, the Old Lincoln County Memorial Commission worked with the Museum of New Mexico to purchase and restore several more properties in town.

These new acquisitions included the old John Tunstall Store, which they bought, restored, and opened as a second museum in 1957.[49] The Commission also purchased the property on which the old Wortley Hotel had stood before burning down in 1936. With assistance from state funds, the commission rebuilt the hotel, opening to the public in

Workers making and stacking adobes during the reconstruction of the Wortley Hotel, 1959
Lincoln County Historical Society

The Courthouse, c.1965
Lincoln County Historical Society

1960. John Boylan oversaw work on all these projects, even managing the Wortley Hotel with his wife beginning in 1962. He and Caroline moved out of the Courthouse curator's apartment in 1960 into the newly renovated James Brent house, also purchased and preserved by the Commission. During the next few years, the commission also acquired the property on which the McSween house originally sat, the Lincoln Pageant Grounds, and Lincoln's first courthouse building, known locally as the Convento. These activities encouraged the commission and local community members to begin the process of nominating the town of Lincoln to be considered for recognition as a National Historic Landmark—a dream that came to reality on December 19, 1960.[50]

In 1962, the New Mexico State Legislature passed a bill authorizing County Commissioners to zone historic districts. The Commission immediately began advocating for leaders in Lincoln County to establish a historic zone protecting the town of Lincoln. Although it would take more than a decade of work to see this dream realized, local advocates and the State Legislature had laid the groundwork. Over the next several years, the stewards of the Courthouse Museum served integral roles in leading the fight for this critical legal protection for Lincoln.[51]

While the Boylans and the Old Lincoln County Memorial Commission focused on other aspects of preservation in Lincoln, the Courthouse Museum remained the primary attraction in town. In 1963, the state legislature passed a bill removing the Old Lincoln County Memorial Commission from under the Museum of New Mexico's jurisdiction.[52] This legislative move further increased the commission's autonomy and ability to manage and maintain the Courthouse Museum as they saw fit. Following John and Nan Boylan's move to the Brent House in 1960, the commission converted the curator's residence into an additional exhibit space. With the curator's quarters no longer needed, the Old Lincoln County Memorial Commission elected to abandon the vault toilets installed by Jerome Hendron and install interior restrooms on the Courthouse's first floor in the southwestern room adjacent to the stairwell. While arguably an improvement over the old vault toilets, the new interior bathrooms took up valuable interpretive space and drastically altered the historical integrity of the building—facts that would eventually lead to their removal. Finally, the commission made the controversial decision to cover the cedar shake roof with asphalt shingles, a significant step backward in attempts to maintain the historical integrity of the building.

Interior of the Frank and Helena Coe Room, 1964
Lincoln County Historical Society

The exhibits displayed in the Courthouse during the 1960s and 1970s changed very little—with one significant exception. On Sunday, July 19, 1964, the Old Lincoln County Memorial Commission opened and dedicated the *Frank and Helena Coe Room* on the Courthouse's second floor in what once served as the county armory. Items in the exhibit included furniture from the Coe Ranch and Frank Coe's percussion cap shotgun that he used alongside Billy the Kid during the Lincoln County War.[53]

In December 1964, John and Nan Boylan took a leave of absence from their positions in Lincoln to tour museums and historical sites in Europe. During their absence, the Old Lincoln County Memorial Commission appointed Edward Penfield, the man from whom they purchased the Tunstall Store in 1957, as temporary curator and custodian of the Lincoln State Monument and Courthouse Museum.[54] The Boylans' sabbatical lasted only half as long as they expected, and they returned to Lincoln in July 1965.[55] Their return did not last long, however, as disagreements with the Secretary-Treasurer of the commission led to a refusal of payment for wages and the need for Nan Boylan to find a new job elsewhere.[56]

Following the Boylans' permanent departure from Lincoln, the commission searched for a new curator. More than ninety local citizens signed a petition requesting that Edward Penfield be named permanent curator for the museum, and several commission members supported this decision. However, the commission eventually chose not to appoint Penfield as the permanent curator, which led to a schism in the community of Lincoln.[57] The commission instead appointed Massachusetts native Paul Gardner to the position in March 1966.[58] Highly educated, Gardner earned a bachelor's degree in architecture from the Massachusetts Institute of Technology, a master's degree in European History at George Washington University, and a master's degree in fine arts from Harvard University. Gardener served as the first Director of the William Rockhill Nelson Museum of Art (now the Nelson-Atkins Museum of Art) in Kansas City, Missouri. During his tenure at the Nelson Museum, Gardner met and befriended artist Peter Hurd and, in 1941, purchased property adjacent to the artist in San Patricio. The year prior, Gardner had assisted Peter Hurd in adapting Phillip Stevenson's play about Billy the Kid and directing its first performance on the grounds of the Courthouse Museum.

When Gardner retired, he split his time between his home in New Mexico and traveling in Europe but briefly came out of retirement in 1966 to run the museums in Lincoln—a position he only intended to occupy until the Commission could find a suitable replacement.[59] Gardner's time as curator lasted only a few months, but he re-established the Courthouse Museum's

Gardner Named Curator At Courthouse Museum

Paul Gardner has assumed his duties as curator-custodian of the Courthouse Museum in Lincoln. These duties include not only the directorship of the Museum, but also the general supervision of the Wortley Hotel, the Tunstall-McSween Store, the Torreon and other historical monuments under the control of the Old Lincoln County Memorial Commission.

Gardner was born in Boston where he attended the local schools and then enrolled at the Massachusetts Institute of Technology to study architecture.

This schooling was interrupted by World War I when he entered the regular army in the Coast Artillery Corps and spent two years of service in France as a captain and was awarded the French Croix de Guerre with palm.

On his return to civilian life he spent several years at George Washington University where he received his B. A. and M. A. in history. Later he attended the Fine Arts Department of Harvard University studying museum directorship and also was awarded an M. A. degree. Additional art history courses were taken at the University of Paris.

In 1931 he was called to Kansas City, Mo., to supervise architectural completion of the William Rockhill Nelson Gallery and to initiate the collections there which now rank among the 10 leading museums of the United States. He was appointed director in 1933.

These duties were interrupted by World War II when in 1942, Gardner was given a leave of absence to join the Allied Military Government. He spent three years in Italy as a lieutenant colonel, supervising the monuments and fine arts section and worked in Naples, Rome, Florence and Genoa.

In 1941, he purchased the Las Milpas ranch at San Patricio as a summer home. The almost

been frequented often by Billy the Kid—was restored entirely and Gardner retired to it when he left the Nelson Gallery in 1953. Since that time, he has spent his winters in Europe and his summers in San Patricio and for several years he has directed the annual pageant, "The Last Escape of Billy the Kid.

Gardner has extensive plans for creating greater interest and attendance at the Courthouse Museum. These include special guided visits for school children, changing small exhibitions to illustrate earlier civilizations such as Egyptian, Greek, Roman, Chinese, etc., and temporary loan exhibitions of all branches of history and art. The Courthouse Museum is open daily and a cordial invitation is extended to everyone.

Demo Enchilada Supper Slated At Bent-Mescalero

Everybody's invited, according to sponsors, to the big enchilada supper and Meet-the-Candidates night at the Bent-Mescalero school Wednesday evening, April 27, for benefit of the Otero county Democratic party.

The festivities start at 5 p.m.

PAUL GARDNER

Alamogordo Daily News
Alamogordo, New Mexico , Sunday, April 24, 1966

Bill and Pat Ward during rehearsals for the "Last Escape of Billy the Kid" Pageant, c.1970. In addition to serving as curators for the Courthouse and Tunstall Museums, the Wards also directed the annual pageant for several years.
Lincoln County Historical Society

temporary exhibit program during his short tenure. On June 5, 1966, the museum opened an art exhibit showcasing the "Natura Sculpture" of Lincoln County resident Wilbur Coe—a staunch supporter of the museum.[60] Following a more exhaustive search for a permanent curator, the commission hired Patricia R. Ward in the fall of 1966. As with previous curators, the Commission hired Ward's husband, Bill, as a part-time employee, continuing the tradition of couples overseeing the operations at the Courthouse Museum.

The Wards arrived in Lincoln during an emerging budget crisis for the State Monument and the Old Lincoln County Memorial Commission. In the late 1960s, the state legislature began steadily decreasing the annual budget for the Lincoln Monument and Courthouse Museum operations and maintenance.[61] Over seventy-five percent of the museum's patrons visited from out of state during this time. Rapidly rising gasoline prices during the early 1970s led to a significant reduction in visitors to Lincoln, forcing the museum to increase admission prices to try and make up the difference needed to maintain the buildings. In 1973, the State Finance Board provided the Commission with an emergency grant of $2,000 to cover the cost of its operations for the year.[62] This need for emergency assistance led to increased conversations regarding the continued management of the Courthouse Museum and the rest of the Lincoln State Monument. In February 1973, the New Mexico State Planning Office received $2,500 from the National Park Service and $6,000 from the Four Corners Regional Commission to conduct a preservation study for the town of Lincoln.[63]

In June 1973, the Old Lincoln County Memorial Commission hosted a meeting at the Wortley Hotel to review the preliminary survey for the study. At the meeting were numerous members of the region's legislative delegation, local community members, and Governor Bruce King.[64] Supporters gathered at the meeting in Lincoln, voicing their concerns and ultimately leading to the expansion of the study and the development of a formal preservation plan for the town. Completed in 1974, *Lincoln, New Mexico: A Plan for Preservation and Growth* included the recommendation that the County Commission consider enacting a preservation ordinance for the Lincoln Historic District National Historic Landmark. The Old Lincoln County Memorial Commission adamantly supported the preservation plan and the ordinance, but financial support for the group from the state continued to diminish.

While undeniably important, the state's investment in studies and plans for preserving Lincoln did not translate directly into funding for the upkeep of the Courthouse Museum and other properties maintained by the Old Lincoln County Memorial Commission. Primarily influenced by this continuing funding crisis, an independent group of successful businessmen and philanthropists decided to take matters into their own hands. In 1975, oilmen Robert Orville Anderson and Joe Lackey, along with artists Peter Hurd, Paul Horgan, and John Meigs, established the Lincoln County Heritage Trust. The men created the organization to preserve "both the

Group Formed To Preserve Historic Southwestern Sites

SAN PATRICIO—The Lincoln County Heritage Trust, a privately funded group with headquarters in San Patricio, N.M., has been formed to preserve historic properties in the Southwest.

Peter Hurd, well known artist and lifetime resident of New Mexico and Lincoln County has been joined by Paul Horgan, author and double recipient of the Pulitzer Prize for history with his books on the Rio Grande and Archbishop Lamy; Robert O. Anderson, rancher, conservationist and Lincoln County resident; Joe Lackey, Roswell civic leader, and John Meigs, artist, author and conservator, have joined the group concerned about the destruction of our rapidly dwindling early buildings and information sources in the Southwest. Conservation is another primary aim of the founders.

The purpose of the Lincoln County Heritage Trust is to investigate the possibilities of preservation and public admission to these properties on a non-profit basis. Their interests are not confined to Lincoln County but cover the entire Southwest. State and national designation of such places as buildings worthy of recognition is a major aim.

At present, the Lincoln County Heritage Trust owns the Montano Store in Lincoln. Present plans call for its opening in early summer as a restored Spanish-American house of the 1860-1880 period. The Trust hopes to work with the state owned and operated properties in Lincoln so that visitors may enjoy Trust and State buildings as a unit. A suggested "one ticket" family admission to all properties has been proposed.

Other interests of the Lincoln County Heritage Trust are the recording and preservation of

material of importance from local and regional sources. Working with the Lincoln County Historical Society, they hope to record interviews, collect documents and early correspondence and copy related materials from other collections. Establishment of a Heritage Trust Press for the publishing of this material is envisioned in the future.

The Trust will actively solicit donations of written material and documents, period and historic furnishings, clothing and artifacts, reflecting the three cultures of the Southwest, Indian, Spanish and Anglo. These are planned for public exhibition.

The Lincoln County Heritage Trust has an extensive library of reference material which will be available to the public on completion of cataloging. This will include periodicals as well as books. Nineteenth century periodicals of all types and 20th century magazines on art and architecture are sought. Several collections of Southwest interest, including Americana such as 19th century quilts and needlework, glass and china, Mexican and New Mexican religious art, paintings and graphics of prominent artists of all periods, including work of Peter Hurd and Henriette Wyeth will be on view in changing exhibitions when suitable housing is obtained. Parts of collections will be available for traveling to smaller communities in the Southwest as well as regional museums.

Public announcements of additional projects will be made as the Lincoln County Heritage Trust completes organization. An advisory committee will be formed to assist the Trust in carrying out its objectives. Rancher Gaylord Freeman of Capitan, is the first appointee selected by the Trust.

Carlsbad Current-Argus
Carlsbad, New Mexico, Sunday, April 10, 1977

The Courthouse, c.1976
Lincoln County Historical Society

architectural and natural beauty of southwestern New Mexico," with a particular interest in the historic town of Lincoln.[65] Their first acquisition in Lincoln came in 1976 when they purchased the historic Montano Store located at the East end of Lincoln—opening the building as a museum in the summer of 1977.[66] The Lincoln County Heritage Trust's move into Lincoln could not have come at a better time. A significant shift in the New Mexico government loomed on the horizon, threatening to end state support for the Courthouse Museum.

Fulfilling a campaign promise, Governor Jerry Apodaca began an aggressive effort to reorganize the New Mexico state government after his election in 1974. After two years of working behind the scenes, Governor Apodaca rolled out his plan during his annual "State of the State" speech on January 20, 1976, and the state legislature approved his plan in March 1977.[67] Even before the official reorganization of state government, legislators attempted to abolish the Old Lincoln County Memorial Commission altogether. A House Bill, sponsored by Representative Able McBride from Bernalillo County, was narrowly defeated during the 1976 legislative session, saving the preservation of the Courthouse for the time being.[68] When the legislature finally authorized Governor Apodaca's reorganization efforts in March 1977, the Courthouse Museum and the Old Lincoln County Memorial Commission again found themselves under the control of the Museum of New

Mexico—itself now part of the newly created Educational, Finance, and Cultural Affairs Department.[69]

With these inevitable changes on the horizon, the Old Lincoln County Memorial Commission elected to take a proactive approach rather than waiting to see what the future had in store for them. Beginning in January 1977, the Commission negotiated with the Lincoln County Heritage Trust regarding transferring operational control of the state properties in Lincoln to the private non-profit entity.[70] At a meeting held on May 10, 1977, the Old Lincoln County Memorial Commission voted to lease "all lands presently owned or to be acquired by the State of New Mexico in the Town of Lincoln" for $1.00 annually to the Lincoln County Heritage Trust. The parties finalized and signed the lease on December 12, 1977. The Lincoln County Heritage Trust officially took over control and operations at the Courthouse Museum in January 1978.[71] Although consulted during this leasing process, the Museum of New Mexico continued to move forward with the implementation of the reorganization, transferring ownership of all artifacts housed in the Courthouse Museum and Tunstall Store from the Old Lincoln County Memorial Commission back to itself during the 1978 legislative session.[72]

Following the election of Governor Bruce King in 1978, the state legislature revisited former governor Jerry Apodaca's reorganization policies, significantly impacting the Old Courthouse Museum and the Old Lincoln County Memorial Commission. In 1979, the Museum of New Mexico regained its autonomy when the legislature voted to remove it from the Department of Education, Finance, and Cultural Affairs. Left out of this move was the Old Lincoln County Memorial Commission, which remained under the oversight of the Department of Education, Finance, and Cultural Affairs and transformed into an advisory committee.[73] This change stripped the Old Lincoln County Memorial Commission of all previous powers. In June 1979, the Museum of New Mexico officially took back control of the Courthouse Museum and the rest of the Lincoln State Monument from the commission, receiving the transfer of operational control from the Lincoln County Heritage Trust on July 1, 1979.[74]

This sudden and drastic change in the operations in Lincoln was nothing less than a direct threat to the continued preservation of the Old Courthouse Museum and the rest of the Lincoln State Monument. When the Museum of New Mexico resumed control of the properties in 1979, they did so with absolutely no legislative budget for operations. During the 1980 legislative session, the Museum of New Mexico requested a $98,100 annual

Renovations Keep Two Historic Lincoln Sites Closed

LINCOLN, N.M. (AP) — Renovations on the historic Wortley Hotel have kept it closed during the tourist season, and work on the Lincoln County Courthouse will close that building during the biggest tourist weekend of the year.

The eight-room hotel has been closed for three months for work on the heating, plumbing, and electrical systems.

Tom Caperton, director of the state Monuments Bureau, said the Wortley should reopen in two or three weeks. The hotel has Lincoln's only restaurant and is the only place to stay overnight.

And the Wortley may not open in time for Old Lincoln Days Aug. 2-4, the town's biggest tourist event.

However, Gary Miller, director of the Lincoln County Heritage Trust, said the closing of the Wortley "seems to have no effect" on tourism. He said attendance at the visitors' center dropped only slightly in June from a year ago.

The Lincoln County Courthouse will close July 22 to begin nine months of extensive renovations that will make it look like it did in the 1890s.

Caperton said the adobe building, built in 1873, has suffered from settling and from bending of the walls.

The Lincoln County Courthouse is best known for a violent escape made by Billy the Kid in 1881.

Caperton said the courthouse closing will benefit tourists because the exhibits housed at the courthouse will be moved to the Tunstall Store, which also is owned by the state.

The Tunstall Store has been open only weekends because of lack of staff, but beginning July 27 it will be open fulltime to allow tourists to see the exhibits, Caperton said.

The state also is looking for a new operator for the Wortley. Tom Garrison, a Texas restaurant owner who held the lease for the hotel since 1982, pulled out two weeks ago, saying he had been losing money.

Carlsbad Current-Argus, Carlsbad, New Mexico, Tuesday, July 09, 1985

budget for the Lincoln State Monument.[75] Although partially funded, State Monuments Director Thomas Caperton continued to appeal to the Museum of New Mexico Board of Regents for additional money, specifically for more staff and much-needed maintenance work in Lincoln—especially for the Courthouse.[76] With limited funding, the State Monument Staff worked to address issues at the site, including the Courthouse Museum. In 1980, the staff closed the building to the public for several months to update the structure's electrical wiring, which had recently failed.[77] With the electrical infrastructure updated, the state purchased new "Custom-made kerosene-style lamps" for the second-floor courtroom the following year. While certainly an improvement to the aesthetics of the space, these lights did little to address the significant structural issues endangering the building.

The Historic Lincoln County Courthouse weathered many storms throughout its history, but in the early 1980s, the irreplaceable building was in danger of being lost. Thankfully, efforts by State Monument staff and local citizens to raise money for the building paid off. In 1982, the state earmarked $346,000 from state-issued severance tax bonds to support a significant restoration project at the Courthouse Museum.[78] Unfortunately, the state never sold the severance tax bonds due to a ruling from the Internal Revenue Service questioning their tax-exempt status. State Monuments Director Thomas Caperton returned to the legislature the following year and successfully gained the appropriation again, which became available in July 1983. Finding a qualified architect, engineer, and contractor delayed the project even further, and restoration work on the Courthouse did not start until 1985. By the time work did commence, increases in material and labor costs

The Courthouse, Lower Level
1985

Former storeroom was divided into restrooms around 1960, and removed during the 1985 rennovation.

Between 1960 and 1985, the entire lower level served as interpretive space for the museum. In 1985, staff removed all furniture, displays, and fixtures in preparation for another major renovation. Contractors also removed the interior public restrooms in 1985 with plans to build new outdoor facilities, which did not happen until 1990.

During the 1985 renovations, contractors removed the doorway added by Jerome Hendron in 1938, returning the staircase to its original configuration.

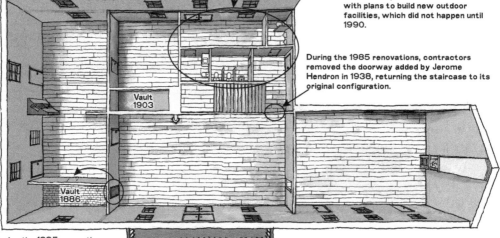

Vault 1903

Vault 1886

During the 1985 renovations, contractors and staff relocated the Diebold Safe, Co. door to its original location along the vault's southern wall.

The balcony had no stairs between 1955 and 1985.

The Courthouse, Upper Level
1985

Formerly James Dolan's bedroom, the courthouse armory, and office space, this room housed the Frank and Helena Coe Room between 1964 and 1985.

Between 1960 and 1985, the entire second floor housed interpretive exhibits related to the Courthouse's history. In 1985, staff removed the exhibits to prepare for major renovations. Contractors installed new exhibits in 1991.

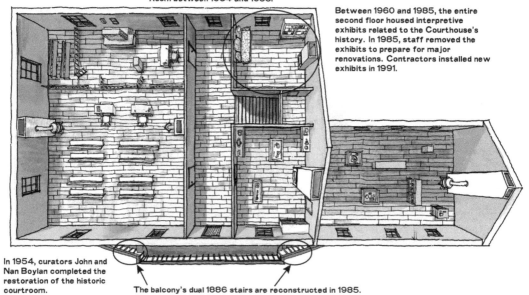

In 1954, curators John and Nan Boylan completed the restoration of the historic courtroom.

The balcony's dual 1886 stairs are reconstructed in 1985.

and further degradation of the building resulted in the original funding amount failing to meet the needs of the building. With the limited funding available, Caperton and his staff had to choose what to tackle first and, in the end, could only accomplish some of what they deemed necessary.[79]

On July 22, 1985, the final major restoration of the Historic Lincoln County Courthouse began. Director Caperton stated that these renovations aimed to restore the Courthouse to what it looked like during the 1890s.[80] For nine months, laborers replastered the exterior of the building, improved roof drainage, repaired windows and doors, added staircases leading from the second-floor balcony, removed the iron security bars from first-floor windows, and constructed a boardwalk around the building. At the same time, contractors removed the asphalt shingles installed in the 1960s, replacing them again with period-appropriate wood shingles.[81] Additional work included the removal of the first-floor bathrooms, reorientating the entrance to the famous stairwell back to its original location, and filling in the north-facing door created by Jerome Hendron in 1939. While workers completed these aesthetic updates, engineers labored to secure the building's structural integrity. Specialists installed massive steel beams between the first and second floors of the building, spanning the entire width of the structure. These beams ensured that the outward spreading of the eighteen-inch-thick adobe walls would never

State Monuments staff building a new fence around the Courthouse Museum, 1992
Lincoln Historic Site Collection

Annual maintenance on the Courthouse Museum, 1991
Lincoln Historic Site Collection

The Historic Lincoln County Courthouse, c.1999
Federal Highway Administration. Office of Planning, Environment, and Realty. Office of Natural and Human Environment. National Scenic Byways Program.

again threaten the structure. Workers also took the opportunity to relocate the massive safe door from its place along the east wall of the former clerk's vault back to its original location on the south-facing wall of the structure. Finally, laborers removed the abandoned vault restrooms built by Jerome Hendron's crew in 1939 to build new restroom facilities further behind the building. Despite these accomplishments, Director Caperton was not satisfied with the total work and returned to the legislature in 1987 to request additional funding for updates to the Courthouse Museum.

One of Caperton's most significant concerns was related to the exhibits in the building. Staff had removed all of the interpretive information and artifacts before the start of the restoration work. Caperton and local staff argued that the exhibits, many installed in the 1940s and 1950s, were outdated and a significant contributor to the museum's recent decline in visitation.[82] Most of the interpretive information was still removed from the museum, aside from one unique new artifact added during the 1985 restoration. While contractors worked on rehabilitating the building, State Monument staff completed a near magical feat—squeezing a full-sized historic stagecoach through the front doors and into place within the Courthouse's main first-floor gallery. The "Mountain Pride" once ran the regular passenger and mail route between Lake Valley, Hillsboro, and Kingston, New

Mexico. Before making its final trip to Lincoln, the "Mountain Pride" had spent decades displayed outside of the New Mexico History Museum in Santa Fe. According to former Lincoln State Monument Head Ranger Jack Rigney, the size of the stagecoach required staff to remove the front door of the Courthouse down to the bare adobe, including the wooden frame. Even after this feat, the "Mountain Pride" only cleared the opening by inches. Other than this new addition, the exhibits in the Courthouse remained outdated or gone altogether.

There was also the issue of restroom facilities at the Courthouse Museum now that contractors had removed the 1960s-era facilities. In 1987 Caperton returned to the state legislature to secure funding for exhibit updates and new detached restrooms. Caperton's request for $134,000.00 to build new accessible facilities at Coronado, Fort Sumner, and Lincoln Historic Sites was slashed by the legislature by more than sixty percent, forcing him to abandon the needed work at both Fort Sumner and Lincoln and use what little money allocated at Coronado State Monument—at that point the most visited state monument. Caperton returned to the legislature the next year and successfully secured the funding needed to finish the renovation and exhibit work at the Courthouse Museum. In 1989, workers added separate restrooms to the lot behind the Courthouse and demolished the seriously damaged storeroom in the southeast corner of the yard.[83] The State Monument Division also contracted with Lynch Museum Services to design and install new exhibits throughout the building, which they completed in 1990.

Since 1990, staff and volunteers at the Lincoln State Monument (now Lincoln Historic Site) have continued efforts to maintain and preserve the Historic Lincoln Courthouse. Thousands of people visit the historic building each year, walking its halls, touching its walls, and continuing to breathe life into the structure. These visitors and the elements take a toll on the nearly 150-year-old building, and the work of its stewards will always be a work in progress. The exterior windows and doors are especially susceptible to the elements, and staff and contractors have sanded and repainted them numerous times over the past three decades.[84] In 2006, the state of New Mexico funded a project to install a modern HVAC system in the Historic Courthouse. Engineers struggled to develop a design that would not destroy the building's historic integrity. The solution to the problem presented itself through the Courthouse's massive brick chimneys. By running the required ductwork from the attic to the first floor through the existing chimney flues, workers avoided adding unsightly and historically inaccurate plumbing.[85]

In the Spring of 2016, a massive hail storm struck the Bonito Valley, causing severe damage to buildings, cars, and much more. The roof of the historic Courthouse took a beating and required significant repairs. After assessing the damage, the State of New Mexico decided that completely replacing the cedar shake roof was the only viable option. In the Spring of 2017, workers with Covenant Solutions completed replacing the roof and refinishing all south-facing windows and doors, using many of the same tools available to George Peppin, Will Dowlin, James Hendron, and many others who preceded them. Finally, in the summer of 2021, Historic Sites staff and master adobe masons with Crocker Limited worked together to refinish the entire interior of the Courthouse. The artisans meticulously patched, replastered, and painted every wall inside the building, finishing with a specially designed clay-based paint developed to emulate historic *gaspe* without the danger of exposing workers or visitors to potentially dangerous materials. At the end of the project, the Courthouse once again looked much as it did in June 1874 when *L.G. Murphy and Co.,* opened its doors for business—and if members of the next generation

The Historic Lincoln County Courthouse, 2019
New Mexico Tourism Department

protect and preserve this invaluable resource as those before them have, visitors will still be able to explore the rooms of the Lincoln County Courthouse for many years to come.

EPILOGUE

For 150 years, the Lincoln County Courthouse had stood vigil over the tiny hamlet of Lincoln, New Mexico, towering above the town's other structures and serving the community in numerous ways. As the store, home, and headquarters of *L.G. Murphy and Company,* "The House" represented the best and worst characteristics of territorial New Mexico—ambition, entrepreneurship, and vision on one side and corruption, greed, and lawlessness on the other. L.G. Murphy, Emil Fritz, James Dolan, and John Riley built an empire based on a ruthless desire for power, guiding their path from their castle-like structure in Lincoln. Their aspirations and methods to obtain them led to violent confrontations with their competitors and to the bloody and costly Lincoln County War. The firm did not survive the conflict, but its headquarters did. Reborn as a beacon of justice in the aftermath of civil unrest, the new Lincoln County Courthouse physically represented a shift in the cultural, political, social, and economic landscape of New Mexico. A movement aimed at transforming New Mexico into a more modern and lawful version of itself, more in line with the progressive path the nation was already on.

The last decades of the nineteenth century were not without incident in Lincoln. The Courthouse played a significant role in several violent episodes, including the now legendary April 28, 1881 escape of Billy the Kid. However, by the dawning of the new century, the building, and much of what it symbolically stood for, was quickly deteriorating. In electing to move the county seat to Carrizozo, Lincoln County's citizens distanced themselves, literally and figuratively, from the frontier image of Lincoln's violent and tumultuous past. The Courthouse building seemed doomed to time, but as Billy the Kid's legendary status rose among the masses, so did calls to preserve the building he made famous as well as the town surrounding it. Since 1939, the Courthouse Museum has anchored one of America's most well-preserved frontier towns, representing what determined efforts to preserve our past can lead to. For generations of visitors, the Lincoln County Courthouse has served as a doorway through time—some famous in name, but most just in search of a connection to the past. To all that walk through the doors of the Lincoln County Courthouse, the building serves as a gateway to the past, a window through which you can see into history and walk in the footsteps of legends. For many, the building will always be known as Billy the Kid's Courthouse. In actuality, the building belongs to us all—standing as a memorial to a transformative and complex time in American history and physical proof that preserving our cultural landscape is a worthwhile and meaningful investment in our collective future.

Billy the Kid's Courthouse: A Timeline

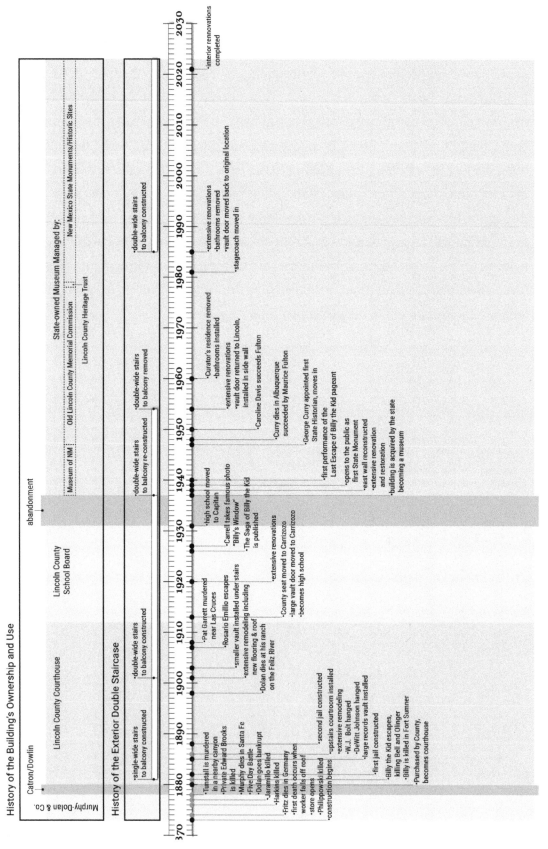

ENDNOTES

Foreward

1 Pat F. Garrett, The Authentic Life of Billy, the Kid: The Noted Desperado of the Southwest, Whose Deeds of Daring and Blood Made His Name a Terror in New Mexico, Arizona and Northern Mexico: A Faithful and Interesting Narrative (Norman, 1967). p. 130.

2 Cozzens, Gary. "A Parting Shot." El Palacio, 2016. https://www.elpalacio.org/2016/09/a-parting-shot/.

3 Burns, Walter Noble. The Saga of Billy the Kid. Garden City, New York: Garden City Publishing Co., INC., 1926. p.35

4 John Sinclair, *Interpretive Panel Drafts*, Lincoln County Historical Society Collection.

5 "Truth About Billy the Kid," *LIFE*, August 4, 1941, pp. 66-69.

6 "It is Not Decay but Peace That Has Settled Over Lincoln," The Albuquerque Tribune, Albuquerque, New Mexico, Thursday, April 21, 1938, www.newspapers.com.

7 *Excerpt from Letter from Robert E. Howard to H.P. Lovecraft,* July 1935. Accessed from https://adventuresfantastic.com/robert-e-howard-in-lincoln-county/

8 Leslie Traylor, "Facts Regarding the Escape of Billy the Kid," Frontier Times, July 1936, 508.

9 "Up in Lincoln," The Albuquerque Journal, Albuquerque, New Mexico, Thursday April 14, 1927, www.newspapers.com.

10 Miguel Antonio Otero et al., *The Real Billy the Kid: With New Light on the Lincoln County War* (Santa Fe: Sunstone Press, 2007), p. 130.

11 The Deming Headlight, Deming, New Mexico, Friday June 18, 1915, www.newspapers.com; "Mrs. Mabry," The Junction City Republic, Junction City, Kansas, Thursday July 25, 1912, www.newspapers.com.

12 "Ms. Katherine Burns Mabry, the only woman lawyer in the state, was admitted to the bar last week," The Albuquerque Morning Journal, Albuquerque, New Mexico, Monday January 15, 1917, www.newspapers.com.

13 Mark J. Dworkin, American Mythmaker: Walter Noble Burns and the Legends of Billy the Kid, Wyatt Earp, and Joaquin Murrieta (Norman: Univ. of Oklahoma Press, 2015). p. 20.

14 "Our Friend Billy the Kid," The Santa Fe New Mexican, Santa Fe, New Mexico, Sunday July 28, 1940, www.newspapers.com

Chapter 1

1 Dutton, Bertha P. 2010. *American Indians of the Southwest*. Albuquerque: University of New Mexico Press.

2 Roberts, Calvin A., and Susan A. Roberts. 2010. *A History of New Mexico*. Albuquerque: University of New Mexico Press.

3 "Annexation," Mississippi Democrat, September 10, 1845, p. 1, www.newspapers.com.

4 "Treaty of Guadalupe Hidalgo (1848)," National Archives and Records Administration (National Archives and Records Administration), accessed July 15, 2022, https://www.archives.gov/milestone-documents/treaty-of-guadalupe-hidalgo#transcript.

5 "Ratified Indian Treaty 261: Apache - Santa Fe, New Mexico Territory, July 1, 1852," National Archives and Records Administration (National Archives and Records Administration), accessed June 10, 2022, https://catalog. archives.gov/id/175192410.

6 "Expedition into the Mescalero Country. Safe Arrival of the Troops. Description of the Country," Santa Fe Weekly Gazette, April 28, 1855, p. 2, www.newspapers.com.

7 Returns From U.S. Military Posts, 1800-1916; Microfilm Publication M617, 1550 rolls; NAID: 561324; Records of the Adjutant General's Office, 1762 - 1984, Record Group 94; The National Archives in Washington, D.C.

8 "Expedition into the Mescalero Country. Safe Arrival of the Troops. Description of the Country," Santa Fe Weekly Gazette, April 28, 1855, p. 2, www.newspapers.com.

9 "Ancestry.com," Returns from U.S. Military Posts, 1800-1916; Microfilm Publication M617, 1550 rolls; NAID: 561324; Records of the Adjutant General's Office, 1762 - 1984, Record Group 94; The National Archives in Washington, D.C. https://www.ancestry.com/search/collections/1571/

10 Frederick W. Nolan, The Lincoln County War: A Documentary History (Santa Fe: Sunstone Press, 2009).

Chapter 2

1 "Ancestry.com," National Archives and Records Administration; Washington, D.C.; Record Group Title: *Records of the AGO, 1762-1984*; Record Group #: *94*; Serie: Register of Enlistments in the United States Army. 1798-1914. *https://www.ancestry.com/search/collections/1198/*

2 National Archives and Records Administration; Washington, D.C.; Record Group Title: *Records of the AGO, 1780s-1917*; Record Group #: *94*; Series Number: *M427*; Roll #: *0015*

3 Frederick W. Nolan, *The Lincoln County War: A Documentary History* (Santa Fe: Sunstone Press, 2009).

4 "Ancestry.com," National Archives and Records Administration (NARA); Washington, D.C.; *Returns from U.S. Military Posts, 1800-1916*; Microfilm Serial: *M617*; Microfilm Roll: *1241*. https://www.ancestry.com/search/collections/1571/

5 *IBID*

6 "Ancestry.com," National Archives and Records Administration (NARA); Washington, D.C.; *Returns from U.S. Military Posts, 1800-1916*; Microfilm Serial: *M617*; Microfilm Roll: *1215*. https://www.ancestry.com/search/collections/1571/

7 "Ancestry.com," *New York, U.S., Arriving Passenger and Immigration Lists, 1820-1850*. https://www.ancestry.com/search/collections/7485/

8 "Ancestry.com," National Archives and Records Administration; Washington, D.C.; Record Group Title: *Records of the AGO, 1762-1984*; Record Group #: *94*; Serie: Register of Enlistments in the United States Army. 1798-1914. *https://www.ancestry.com/search/collections/1198/*

9 "Arrival of Major Carlton's Dragoons," Santa Fe Weekly Post, June 17, 1854, p. 2, www.newspapers.com.

10 "Ancestry.com," National Archives and Records Administration (NARA); Washington, D.C.; *Returns from U.S. Military Posts, 1800-1916*; Microfilm Serial: *M617*; Microfilm Roll: *1257*. https://www.ancestry.com/search/collections/1571/

11 "Ancestry.com," Office of the Adjutant General. Military Records, 1850–1942. Military Dept., Adjutant General's Office Records (1850–1944), ID Number R186. California State Archives, Office of the Secretary of State, Sacramento, California. https://www.ancestry.com/search/collections/8807/

12 "Ancestry.com," National Archives and Records Administration (NARA); Washington, D.C.; *Returns from U.S. Military Posts, 1800-1916*; Microfilm Serial: *M617*; Microfilm Roll: *1241*, https://www.ancestry.com/search/collections/1571/

13 "Ancestry.com," National Archives and Records Administration (NARA); Washington, D.C.; *Returns from U.S. Military Posts, 1800-1916*; Microfilm Serial: *M617*; Microfilm Roll: *13*, https://www.ancestry.com/search/collections/1571/

14 *IBID*

15 Condition of the Indian Tribes: Report of the Joint Special Committee, Appointed under Joint Resolution of March 3, 1865: With an Appendix. (Washington: G.P.O., 1867), 200.

16 "Sutlers at Military Posts," Weekly New Mexican, March 17, 1868, p. 1, www.newspapers.com.

17 Weekly New Mexican, May 11, 1866, p. 2, www.newspapers.com.

18 "Ancestry.com," The National Archives and Records Administration; Washington, D.C.; Internal Revenue Assessment Lists for the Territory of New Mexico, 1862-1870, 1872-1874; Series: M782; Roll: 1; Description: Annual Lists; Apr 1869; Record Group: 58, Records of the Internal Revenue Service, 1791 - 2006. https://www.ancestry.com/search/collections/1264/

19 Frederick W. Nolan, *The Lincoln County War: A Documentary History* (Santa Fe: Sunstone Press, 2009), Pg. 38.

20 "Fold3.com," *Letter from L.G. Murphy to Secretary of War William Belknap*, July 22, 1873, Letters Received by the Office of the Adjutant General, Main Series, 1871-1880. https://www.fold3.com/publication/814/letters-received-by-the-adjutant-general-1871-1880

21 Wallace, Andrew. "Duty in the District of New Mexico: A Military Memoir." New Mexico Historical Review 50, 3 (2021). https://digitalrepository.unm.edu/nmhr/vol50/iss3/4. Pg. 243

22 Lily Klasner, John Simpson Chisum, and Eve Ball, My Girlhood among Outlaws (Tucson, AZ: University of Arizona Press, 1988).

23 "Dissolution Notice," The Santa Fe New Mexican Santa Fe, December 28, 1869, p.2, www.newspapers.com.

24 "Ancestry.com," National Archives and Records Administration; Washington, D.C.; Record Group Title: Records of the AGO, 1762-1984; Record Group #: 94; Serie: Register of Enlistments in the United States Army. 1798-1914. https://www.ancestry.com/search/collections/1198/

25 Santa Fe Weekly Post, April 3, 1869, p.2, www.newspapers.com

26 "County Officers," The Santa Fe New Mexican Santa Fe, July 21, 1869, p.1, www.newspapers.com

27 "Albuquerque Correspondence," The Santa Fe New Mexican August 26, 1870, p.1, www.newspapers.com.

28 The Santa Fe New Mexican October 31, 1870, p.1, www.newspapers.com.

29 "Fold3.com," *Letter from Captain James Randlett to Secretary of War William Belknap, July 22, 1873*, Letters Received by the Office of the Adjutant General, Main Series, 1871-1880. https://www.fold3.com/publication/814/letters-received-by-the-adjutant-general-1871-1880

30 Mehren, Lawrence L. "A History of the Mescalero Apache Reservation, 1869-1881." Thesis, The University of Arizona, 1968. p.30

31 Frederick W. Nolan, *The Lincoln County War: A Documentary History* (Santa Fe: Sunstone Press, 2009). pp. 482-483

32 Mehren, Lawrence L. "A History of the Mescalero Apache Reservation, 1869-1881." Thesis, The University of Arizona, 1968. p.35.

33 "The Territories," The Santa Fe New Mexican, February 7, 1873, p.1, www.newspapers.com.

34 "Ancestry.com," National Archives and Records Administration (NARA); Washington, D.C.; *Returns from U.S. Military Posts, 1800-1916*; Microfilm Serial: *M617*; Microfilm Roll: *1306*, https://www.ancestry.com/search/collections/1571/.

35 "Fold3.com," *Letter from Captain James Randlett to Secretary of War William Belknap, July 22, 1873*, Letters Received by the Office of the Adjutant General, Main Series, 1871-1880. https://www.fold3.com/publication/814/letters-received-by-the-adjutant-general-1871-1880.

36 Mehren, Lawrence L. "A History of the Mescalero Apache Reservation, 1869-1881." Thesis, The University of Arizona, 1968. p.55.

37 Mehren, Lawrence L. "A History of the Mescalero Apache Reservation, 1869-1881." Thesis, The University of Arizona, 1968. p.54.

38 Weekly New Mexican, May 13, 1873, p.2, www.newspapers.com

39 "Fold3.com," *Letter from Captain James Randlett to Secretary of War William Belknap, July 22, 1873*, Letters Received by the Office of the Adjutant General, Main Series, 1871-1880. https://www.fold3.com/publication/814/letters-received-by-the-adjutant-general-1871-1880.

40 "Fold3.com," *Letter from Captain James Randlett to Adjutant General Edward D. Townsend*, Letters Received by the Office of the Adjutant General, Main Series, 1871-1880. https://www.fold3.com/publication/814/letters-received-by-the-adjutant-general-1871-1880.

41 "Fold3.com," *Letter from Captain James Randlett to Lt. James Wilkinson, October 16, 1873*, Letters Received by the Office of the Adjutant General, Main Series, 1871-1880. https://www.fold3.com/publication/814/letters-received-by-the-adjutant-general-1871-1880.

42 "Fold3.com," *Order from Warren Bristol to J. Gylam*, Letters Received by the Office of the Adjutant General, Main Series, 1871-1880. https://www.fold3.com/publication/814/letters-received-by-the-adjutant-general-1871-1880.

43 Mehren, Lawrence L. "A History of the Mescalero Apache Reservation, 1869-1881." Thesis, The University of Arizona, 1968. p.54.

44 *Annual Report of the Commissioner of Indian Affairs to the Secretary of the Interior for the Year 1873* (Washington: G.P.O., 1873). P.264.

45 "Indenture between Murphy, Fritz, and Edwin Dudley for Post Sutler Store $8,000.00," June 13, 1873. Lincoln County Deed Book A, pp. 79-80.

46 *Annual Report of the Commissioner of Indian Affairs to the Secretary of the Interior for the Year 1873* (Washington: G.P.O., 1873). P.264.

Chapter 3

1 The Santa Fe New Mexican, May 22, 1874, p.1, www.newspapers.com.

2 "Ancestry.com," Department of Commerce and Labor, Bureau of the Census. Official Register of the United States, Containing a List of the Officers and Employees in the Civil, Military, and Naval Service. Digitized books (77 volumes). Oregon State Library, Salem, Oregon. https://www.ancestry.com/search/collections/2525/.

3 Frederick W. Nolan, *The Lincoln County War: A Documentary History* (Santa Fe: Sunstone Press, 2009). Page 47

4 "L.G. Murphy and Co., Wholesale and Retail Dealers in General Merchandise." The Santa Fe New Mexican, January 21, 1874, p.3, www.newspapers.com.

5 Letter from John Newcomb to Commissioner of General Land Office, unknown date. Lincoln Historic Site Archives.

6 Letter from John Newcomb to Commissioner of General Land Office, December 2, 1876. Lincoln Historic Site Archives.

7 L. G. Murphy & Co. ledger, May 1873–January, 1874, Special Collections, University of Arizona, Tucson, Arizona.

8 The National Archives in Washington D.C.; Record Group: Records of the Bureau of the Census; Record Group Number: 29; Series Number: M653; Residence Date: 1860; Home in 1860: Santa Fe, Santa Fe, New Mexico Territory; Roll: M653_714; Page: 487; Family History Library Film: 803714. https://www.ancestry.com/imageviewer/collections/7667/images/4235198_00131?pId=54603056

9 Ancestry.com," National Archives and Records Administration (NARA); Washington, D.C.; *Returns from U.S. Military Posts, 1800-1916*; Microfilm Serial: *M617*; Microfilm Roll: *261*. https://www.ancestry.com/imageviewer/collections/1571/images/32169_125945-00268?pId=6470973

10 Lily Klasner, John Simpson Chisum, and Eve Ball, My Girlhood among Outlaws (Tucson, AZ: University of Arizona Press, 1988).

11 L. G. Murphy & Co. ledger, May 1873–January, 1874, Special Collections, University of Arizona, Tucson, Arizona.

12 "The Late Major L.G. Murphy," Weekly New Mexican, October 26, 1878, p.2, www.newspapers.com.

Chapter 4

1 "Affray in Lincoln County," The Santa Fe New Mexican, November 6, 1874, p.1, www.newspapers.com.

2 "Fatal Accident at Lincoln," The Santa Fe New Mexican, September 11, 1876, p.1, www.newspapers.com.

3 "The Lincoln County Tragedies," Weekly New Mexican, May 22, 1877, p.1, www.newspapers.com.

4 "Attorneys," The Eureka Herald and Greenwood County Republican, May 7, 1874, p.1, www.newspapers.com.

5 "McSween and Murphy Warranty Deed," February 9, 1873. Lincoln County Deed Book A.

6 "Articles of incorporation between J.J. Dolan and John H. Riley." Lincoln County Deed Book B. pp. 19-22.

7 "Gov. Axtell in Lincoln," The Santa Fe New Mexican, May 24, 1876, p.1, www.newspapers.com.

8 "Mortgage Contract Between Thomas Catron and J.J. Dolan and John Riley," Lincoln County Contracts Book B, pp.110-114.

9 "The Lincoln County War," The Mesilla Valley Independent, May 11, 1878, p.1, www.newspapers.com.

10 R.M Barron, and Leon C. Metz, Lt. Col. N.A.M. Dudley Court of Inquiry, Fort Stanton, New Mexico 1879, (El Paso, TX) p. 108.

11 "Notice," Weekly New Mexican, Santa Fe, New Mexico, Sat, Jul 13, 1878, p.2, www.newspapers.com.

12 "Transfer of Property from J.J. Dolan and John Riley to Will Dowlin & Co.," January 5, 1879, Lincoln County Contracts Book B, pp.241-243.

13 Las Vegas Weekly, June 30, 1877, p.4, www.newspapers.com.

14 "From Lincoln," Santa Fe New Mexican, March 10, 1881, p.3, www.newspapers.com.

Chapter 5

1 "Ancestry.com," National Archives and Records Administration (NARA); Washington, D.C.; *Record of Appointment of Postmasters, 1832-Sept. 30, 1971*; Roll #: *84*; Archive Publication #: *M841*

2 Commissioners Journal of Proceedings, Book A: 79, https://www.ancestry.com/search/collections/1932/.

3 Redfield, Georgia B. Mrs. Amelia (Bolton) Church. Other. Accessed June 13, 2022. https://memory.loc.gov/mss/wpalh1/19/1917/19170505/19170505.pdf.

4 Lincoln County Commissioners Journal of Proceedings, Book A: p.78

5 "Escape of Billy the Kid," The York Daily York, May 5, 1881, p.4, www.newspapers.com.

6 "Those Who Say Billy Wasn't Fast, Never Saw Him Draw," Alamogordo Daily News, August 7, 1957, p.6, www.newspapers.com.

7 Lincoln County Commissioners Journal of Proceedings, Book A, p. 125

8 Lincoln County Commissioners Journal of Proceedings, Book A, pg. 78.

9 Lincoln County Commissioners Journal of Proceedings, Book A, pp. 88-89.

10 Lincoln County Commissioners Journal of Proceedings, Book A, pp. 87-88,95,101.

11 "Official Vote of Lincoln County," The Lincoln County Leader, November 18, 1882, p.2, www.newspapers.com.

12 Lincoln County Commissioners Journal of Proceedings, Book A, pp. 80-81; 84-85.

13 Lincoln County Commissioners Journal of Proceedings, Book A, p.89.

14 Lincoln County Commissioners Journal of Proceedings, Book A, p. 92.

15 "Gazette Gleanings," The Las Vegas Daily Gazette, September, 20 1881, p.4, www.newspapers.com.

16 Lincoln County Commissioners Journal of Proceedings, Book A, p. 98.

17 Lincoln County Commissioners Journal of Proceedings, Book A, pp. 113-114.

Chapter 6

1 "County Commissioners' Report," The Lincoln County Leader, November 11, 1882, p.2, www.newspapers.com.

2 "Reminisces of Lincoln County and White Oaks by Old Sages and Stagers, No. XIV by G. Gauss," The Lincoln County Leader, March 1, 1890, p.1, www.newspapers.com.

3 Lincoln County Commissioners Journal of Proceedings, Book A, pp.94-95.

4 Poe, Sophie A. *Buckboard Days*. Albuquerque: University of New Mexico Press, 1981, p.205

5 Lincoln County Commissioners Journal of Proceedings, Book A, p.149.

6 Poe, Sophie A. *Buckboard Days*. Albuquerque: University of New Mexico Press, 1981, p.212

7 Poe, Sophie A. *Buckboard Days*. Albuquerque: University of New Mexico Press, 1981, p.205

8 Poe, Sophie A. *Buckboard Days*. Albuquerque: University of New Mexico Press, 1981, p.205

9 "Proceedings of the Board of County Commissioners," Lincoln County Leader, January 20, 1883, p.2, www.newspapers.com.

10 Poe, Sophie A. *Buckboard Days*. Albuquerque: University of New Mexico Press, 1981, p.206

11 Lincoln County Commissioners Journal of Proceedings, Book A, pp.134, 155.

12 Lincoln County Commissioners Journal of Proceedings, Book A, pp.134, 167.

13 Lincoln County Commissioners Journal of Proceedings, Book A, pp.226-227.

14 Lincoln County Commissioners Journal of Proceedings, Book A, pp.125, 268.

15 The Lincoln County Leader, August 21, 1886, p.4, www.newspapers.com.

16 "Commissioners Proceedings," White Oaks Eagle, August 1, 1901, p.7, www.newspapers.com.

17 Lincoln County Commissioners Journal of Proceedings, Book A, p.224.

18 "Local Political Potpourri," The Lincoln County Leader, November 1, 1884, p.1, www.newspapers.com.

19 Lincoln County Commissioners Journal of Proceedings, Book A, p.316.

20 "County Commissioner's Report," The Lincoln County Leader, November 11, 1882, p.2

21 "Louisiana State University Annual Graduation Exercises," The Times-Picayune, June 30, 1872, p.12; "Ancestry.com," Year: 1880; Census Place: White Oaks, Lincoln, New Mexico; Roll: 802; Family History Film: 1254802; Page: 413D; Enumeration District: 058; Image: 0836

22 "Local Roundups," The Lincoln County Leader, November 26, 1887, p.4, www.newspapers.com.

23 "Lincoln Laconics," The Lincoln County Leader, April 14, 1883, p.4, www.newspapers.com.

24 Lincoln County Commissioners Journal of Proceedings, Book A, p.296, www.newspapers.com; "Lincoln County, Albuquerque Morning Democrat, June 3, 1886, p.3, www.newspapers.com.

25 "Items of Interest from In and Around the Garden City of New Mexico," Las Cruces Sun-News, June 2, 1894, p.1, www.newspapers.com.

26 White Oaks Eagle, July 30, 1896, p.2, www.newspapers.com.

27 Lincoln County Commissioners Journal of Proceedings, Book A, p.296.

28 "Points from Lincoln," Lincoln County Leader, March 3, 1883, p.4, www.newspapers.com.

29 "Republican County Convention," Lincoln County Leader, March 8, 1884, p.1, www.newspapers.com; "People's Convention, Lincoln County Leader, October 4, 1884, p.4, www.newspapers.com.

30 Lincoln County Commissioners Journal of Proceedings, Book A, p.316.

31 "Marriage of Sheriff James Brent," The Lincoln County Leader, July 3, 1886, p.1, www.newspapers.com.

Chapter 7

1 Poe, Sophie A. *Buckboard Days*. Albuquerque: University of New Mexico Press, 1981, p.206

2 "William James Bolt Expiates His Foul Crime with His Life," The Lincoln County Leader, June 26, 1886, p.1, www.newspapers.com.

3 "Yank'd," The Lincoln County Leader, November 27, 1886, p.1, www.newspapers.com.

4 Lincoln County Commissioners Journal of Proceedings, Book A, p.296.

5 "William James Bolt Expiates His Foul Crime with His Life," The Lincoln County Leader, June 26, 1886, p.1, www.newspapers.com.

6 "Yank'd,"The Lincoln County Leader, November 27, 1886, p.1, www.newspapers.com.

7 "Prisoners Recaptured," The Las Vegas Gazette, January 31, 1883, p.4, www.newspapers.com.

8 "That Lynching Affair," The Lincoln County, February 17, 1883, p.2, www.newspapers.com.

9 Poe, Sophie A. *Buckboard Days*. Albuquerque: University of New Mexico Press, 1981, p.234-235.

10 "For Two Murders," The New Mexican Review, July 23, 1885, p.3, www.newspapers.com.

11 "Territorial Legislature," The New Mexican, March 20, 1884, p.3, www.newspapers.com.

12 "A Criminal Celebrity," The New Mexican Review, February 5, 1885, p.3, www.newspapers.com.

13 "For Two Murders," The New Mexican Review, July 23, 1885, p.3, www.newspapers.com.

14 "Court Chronicles," The Santa Fe New Mexican, September 26, 1885, p.1, www.newspapers.com.

15 "Convicted of Murder," The Roswell Daily Record, May 8, 1905, p.3, www.newspapers.com.

16 "Lincoln County Court," Las Vegas Daily Optic, May 10, 1905, p.5, www.newspapers.com.

17 "To be Hanged at Lincoln This Month," The Roswell Daily Record, March 5, 1907, p.1, www.newspapers.com.

18 "Woman to Plead for Life of Brother," Albuquerque Journal, March 9, 1907, p.2, www.newspapers.com.

19 "Jail Delivery at Lincoln," The Roswell Daily Record, May 7, 1907, p.1, www.newspapers.com.

Chapter 8

1 Lincoln County Commissioners Journal of Proceedings, Book A, p.237.

2 "Local Roundups," The Lincoln County Leader, July 11, 1885, p.4, www.newspapers.com.

3 Lincoln County Commissioners Journal of Proceedings, Book A, p.296.

4 "Local Roundups," The Lincoln County Leader, July 11, 1885, p.4, www.newspapers.com.

5 Lincoln County Commissioners Journal of Proceedings, Book A, pp. 296, 314.

6 Lincoln County Commissioners Journal of Proceedings, Book C, pp. 7,11.

7 Lincoln County Commissioners Journal of Proceedings, Book A, p.296.

8 Lincoln County Commissioners Journal of Proceedings, Book A, p.299.

9 "From our Thursday Friday," The Lincoln County Leader, June 9, 1888, p.1, www.newspapers.com.

10 Lincoln County Commissioners Journal of Proceedings, Book A, p.411.

11 Lincoln County Commissioners Journal of Proceedings, Book A, p.447.

12 Lincoln County Commissioners Journal of Proceedings, Book A, p.457.

13 Lincoln County Commissioners Journal of Proceedings, Book C, p.77.

14 "Tax Levy," White Oaks Eagle, July 26, 1900, p.2, www.newspapers.com.

15 Lincoln County Commissioners Journal of Proceedings, Book C, p.145.

16 "Bids for Courthouse Repairs," White Oaks Eagle, August 1, 1901, p.5, www.newspapers.com.

17 "Personal Mention," White Oaks Eagle, February 28, 1901, p.3, www.newspapers.com.

18 "Capitan News," White Oaks Eagle, October 24, 1901, p.7, www.newspapers.com.

19 Lincoln County Commissioners Journal of Proceedings, Book D, p.7.

20 Lincoln County Commissioners Journal of Proceedings, Book D, p.8.

21 Henn Archives, Lincoln, New Mexico, Plaintiff Exhibit No. 4 Filed March 26, 1910.

Chapter 9

1 "Ancestry.com," *1860 United States Federal Census*, NARA microfilm publication M653, 1,438 rolls. Washington, D.C.: National Archives and Records Administration, n.d.

2 "Ancestry.com," *1900 United States Federal Census*, United States of America, Bureau of the Census. *Twelfth Census of the United States, 1900*. Washington, D.C.: National Archives and Records Administration, 1900. T623, 1854 rolls.

3 "Cloudcroft," The New Mexican Review, August 24, 1899, p.3, www.newspapers.com.

4 "From Angus," White Oaks Eagle, March 28, 1901, p.2, www.newspapers.com.

5 "County Division," White Oaks Eagle, February 19, 1903, p.4, www.newspapers.com.

6 "Carrizozo the County Seat," Carrizozo News, July 9, 1909, p.1, www.newspapers.com.

7 "The County Seat Movement," Carrizozo News, June 11, 1909, p.1, www.newspapers.com.

8 "Against Removal of the County Seat," Carrizozo News, August 13, 1909, p.8, www.newspapers.com.

9 "Carrizozo Wins by Overwhelming Majority," Carrizozo News, August 20, 1909, p.1, www.newspapers.com.

10 "County Seat Muddle," Carrizozo News, July 14, 1911, p.6, www.newspapers.com.

11 Operations Begun," Carrizozo News, March 25, 1910, p.6, www.newspapers.com; "Ancient Legal Squabble Takes Another Turn," Albuquerque Morning Journal, October 7, 1915, p.3, www.newspapers.com.

12 "Gray v. Taylor, 227 U.S. 51 (1913)." Justia Law. Accessed July 16, 2022.

https://supreme.justia.com/cases/federal/us/227/51/.

13 "Ancient Legal Squabble Takes Another Turn," Albuquerque Morning Journal, October 7, 1915, p.3, www. newspapers.com.

14 "Lincoln County Scene of Exciting Early Day Events," Carrizozo Outlook, March 32, 1917, p.5, www. newspapers.com.

15 "Third Degree Method to be Abolished by Whetmore Bill," Albuquerque Morning Journal, January 27, 1917, p.1, www.newspapers.com.

16 "Commissioners" Proceedings," Carrizozo Outlook, October 17, 1919, p.10, www.newspapers.com.

17 "Board of Education," Carrizozo Outlook, April 9, 1920, p.3, www.newspapers.com.

18 Thomas J. Caperton, Historic Structure Report Lincoln State Monument Lincoln, New Mexico, 1983. p. 555.

19 "New School Building for Lincoln," Carrizozo Outlook, July 9, 1920, p.3, www.newspapers.com.

20 *Report to Dr. R. G. Fisher on the Restoration of the Old Lincoln County Courthouse for the Week Ending April, 8, 1938.* Jerome Hendron, Lincoln County Historical Society Collection.

21 Thomas J. Caperton, Historic Structure Report Lincoln State Monument Lincoln, New Mexico, 1983. p. 555.

22 *Report to Dr. R. G. Fisher on the Restoration of the Old Lincoln County Courthouse for the Week Ending April, 8, 1938.* Jerome Hendron, Lincoln County Historical Society Collection.

Chapter 10

1 "Ancestry.com," Year: 1940; Census Place: Lincoln, Lincoln, New Mexico; Roll: m-t0627-02447; Page: 3B; Enumeration District: 14-1.

2 *Excerpt from Letter from Robert E. Howard to H.P. Lovecraft,* July 1935. Accessed from https://adventuresfantastic.com/robert-e-howard-in-lincoln-county/

3 "Restored Tower to be Dedicated Today in Lincoln," Albuquerque Journal, February 24, 1935, p.7, www. newspapers.com.

4 "Lincoln Courthouse Considered as a Park," Albuquerque Journal, March 28, 1937, p.1, www.newspapers.com.

5 "Tangle on School Bill," Albuquerque Journal, February 11, 1937, p.4, www.newspapers.com.

6 "Henn Archives," Box 143, *Lincoln Buildings Studies Caperton rewrite 1979.*

7 "Henn Archives," Box 143, *Lincoln Buildings Studies Caperton rewrite 1979.*

8 "Senate Bills Introduced," The Albuquerque Tribune, February 11, 1937, p.3, www.newspapers.com.

9 "Bills Passed by House," Clovis News-Journal, February 23, 1937, p.8, www.newspapers.com.

10 Lincoln County Deeds Book A-17, p.448; "State Monument Projects," *El Palacio Volume XLV*, December, 1938 Pg. 110.

11 "FDR Approves Rebuilding of Lincoln Jail," The Albuquerque Tribune, February 7, 1938, p.2, www. newspapers.com.

12 J.W. Hendron, *The Restoration of the Old Lincoln County Courthouse at Lincoln, New Mexico*, Museum of New Mexico, Works Progress Administration, 1938-1939, p.17.

13 Jerome Hendron, "The Old Lincoln Courthouse," *El Palacio Volume XLVI*, January, 1939, p.2.

14 "Lincoln Courthouse Being Remolded to Restore 'War' Touch," Albuquerque Journal, April 11, 1938, p.7, www.newspapers.com.

Chapter 11

1 J.W. Hendron, *The Restoration of the Old Lincoln County Courthouse at Lincoln, New Mexico*, Museum of New Mexico, Works Progress Administration, 1938-1939, p.18.

2 *Report to Dr. R. G. Fisher on the Restoration to the Old Lincoln County Courthouse for the Week Ending April, 16, 1938.* Jerome Hendron, Lincoln County Historical Society Collection.

3 *IBID April, 8, 1938.*

4 *IBID April, 23, 1938.*

5 *IBID April, 30, 1938.*

6 J.W. Hendron, *The Restoration of the Old Lincoln County Courthouse at Lincoln, New Mexico*, Museum of New Mexico, Works Progress Administration, 1938-1939.

7 *Report to Dr. R. G. Fisher on the Restoration to the Old Lincoln County Courthouse for the Week Ending April, 23, 1938.* Jerome Hendron, Lincoln County Historical Society Collection.

8 J.W. Hendron, *The Restoration of the Old Lincoln County Courthouse at Lincoln, New Mexico*, Museum of New Mexico, Works Progress Administration, 1938-1939.

9 IBID, p.12.

10 *Report to Dr. R. G. Fisher on the Restoration to the Old Lincoln County Courthouse for the Week Ending May, 14, 1938.* Jerome Hendron, Lincoln County Historical Society Collection.

11 J.W. Hendron, *The Restoration of the Old Lincoln County Courthouse at Lincoln, New Mexico*, Museum of New Mexico, Works Progress Administration, 1938-1939.

12 *Report to Dr. R. G. Fisher on the Restoration to the Old Lincoln County Courthouse for the Week Ending June, 18, 1938.* Jerome Hendron, Lincoln County Historical Society Collection.

13 *IBID June, 25, 1938.*

14 *IBID July, 9, 1938.*

15 *IBID July, 16, 1938.*

16 *RIBID July, 16, 1938.*

17 *IBID July, 23, 1938.*

18 *IBID August, 13, 1938.*

19 *IBID Ending August, 27, 1938.*

20 *IBID September, 3, 1938.*

21 *IBID September 17, 1938.*

22 *IBID October 1, 1938.*

23 J.W. Hendron, *The Restoration of the Old Lincoln County Courthouse at Lincoln, New Mexico*, Museum of New Mexico, Works Progress Administration, 1938-1939.

24 IBID, p.5.

25 *Report to Dr. R. G. Fisher on the Restoration to the Old Lincoln County Courthouse for the Week Ending October 1, 1938.* Jerome Hendron, Lincoln County Historical Society Collection.

26 J.W. Hendron, *The Restoration of the Old Lincoln County Courthouse at Lincoln, New Mexico*, Museum of New Mexico, Works Progress Administration, 1938-1939, p.6.

27 *Report to Dr. R. G. Fisher on the Restoration to the Old Lincoln County Courthouse for the Week Ending December 17, 1938.* Jerome Hendron, Lincoln County Historical Society Collection.

28 *IBID October 22, 1938.*

29 *IBID October 29, 1938.*

30 *IBID December, 3, 1938.*

31 *IBID December 17, 1, 1938.*

32 *IBID December, 24, 1938.*

33 *Jerome Hendron letter to Reginald Fisher*, January 22, 1976, Sinclair papers, University of New Mexico Center for Southwest Research

34 *Report to Dr. R. G. Fisher on the Restoration to the Old Lincoln County Courthouse for the Week Ending January, 28, 1939.* Jerome Hendron, Lincoln County Historical Society Collection.

35 *Jerome Hendron Letter to Reginald Fisher,* March 24, 1939, Lincoln County Historical Society Collection.

36 *Report to Dr. R. G. Fisher on the Restoration to the Old Lincoln County Courthouse for the Week Ending October, 29, 1938.* Jerome Hendron, Lincoln County Historical Society Collection.

37 *Jerome Hendron Letter to Reginald Fisher,* April 10, 1939, Lincoln County Historical Society Collection.

38 *Jerome Hendron Letter to Reginald Fisher,* April 22, 1939, Lincoln County Historical Society Collection.

39 *Jerome Hendron Letter to Reginald Fisher,* March 30, 1939, Lincoln County Historical Society Collection.

40 *Jerome Hendron Letter to Reginald Fisher,* May 5, 1939, Lincoln County Historical Society Collection.

41 J.W. Hendron, *The Restoration of the Old Lincoln County Courthouse at Lincoln, New Mexico*, Museum of New Mexico, Works Progress Administration, 1938-1939, p.6; *Albert Ely Letter to Jerome Hendron,* April 4, 1939, Lincoln County Historical Society Collection.

42 J.W. Hendron, *The Restoration of the Old Lincoln County Courthouse at Lincoln, New Mexico*, Museum of New Mexico, Works Progress Administration, 1938-1939, p.8.

43 *Jerome Hendron Letter to Reginald Fisher,* May 16, 1939, Lincoln County Historical Society Collection.

44 *Report to Dr. R. G. Fisher on the Restoration to the Old Lincoln County Courthouse for the Week Ending May, 20, 1938.* Jerome Hendron, Lincoln County Historical Society Collection.; *Works Progress Administration Project Proposal*, Old Lincoln County Courthouse, December 20, 1937, Lincoln County Historical Society Collection.

45 *Jerome Hendron Letter to Reginald Fisher,* March 30, 1939, Lincoln County Historical Society Collection.

46 *Albert Ely Letter to Jerome Hendron,* April 4, 1939, Lincoln County Historical Society Collection.

47 *Jerome Hendron Letter to Reginald Fisher,* May 16, 1939, Lincoln County Historical Society Collection.

48 *Reginald Fisher Letter to Senator Perry Sears,* June 18, 1939, Lincoln County Historical Society Collection.

49 "From the State Papers," The Santa Fe New, August 8, 1939, p.4, www.newspapers.com.

50 Jerome Hendron, "The Old Lincoln Courthouse," *El Palacio Volume XLVI*, January, 1939.

51 *Old Courthouse Dedication Program*, Lincoln County Historical Society Collection.

Chapter 12

1 *Albert Ely Letter to Jerome Hendron*, March 21, 1939, Lincoln County Historical Society Collection.

2 "John Sinclair Named Custodian of Museum," The Albuquerque Tribune, May 8, 1940, p.6, www.newspapers.com.

3 Ben E. Pingenot, *Review of A Cowboy Writer in New Mexico: The Memoirs of John L. Sinclair by John Sinclair*, Great Plains Quarterly, Spring 1998.

4 John Sinclair, *Sinclair Memoirs*, Sinclair papers, University of New Mexico Center for Southwest Research.

5 *Letter to John Sinclair to Unknown Museum of New Mexico Staff Member*, June 7, 1940, Lincoln County Historical Society Collection.

6 "Mountain Resort of Ruidoso Enjoys Largest Summer Season of Many Years," El Paso Times, November 16, 1941, p. 72.

7 John Sinclair, *Sinclair Memoirs*, Sinclair papers, University of New Mexico Center for Southwest Research.

8 "State News in Brief," The Santa Fe New Mexican, April 23, 1936, p.4, www.newspapers.com.

9 Billy the Kid to Ride Again as Coronado Feature," Las Cruces Sun-News, June 17, 1940, p.1, www.newspapers.com.

10 "Old Lincoln to be Scene of Gay Fiesta," The Albuquerque Tribune, June 18, 1940, p.4, www.newspapers.com.

11 Henn Archives, *Custodians and Curators*, p.143.

12 *John Sinclair letter to Molly Madden*, January 22, 1976, Sinclair papers, University of New Mexico Center for Southwest Research; *John Sinclair letter to Albert G. Ely*, October 19, 1942, Lincoln County Historical Society Collection.

13 *Western Union Telegram*, Sinclair papers, University of New Mexico Center for Southwest Research.

14 "Ancestry.com." *U.S., World War II Draft Cards Young Men, 1940-1947* [database on-line]. Lehi, UT, USA: Ancestry.com Operations, Inc., 2011.

15 Henn Archives, *Custodians and Curators*, p.144.

16 "Ex-Governor Curry is State Historian," The Gallup Independent, April 12, 1945, p.10, www.newspapers.com.

17 "Curry to Perpetuate Memory of Pioneers," Albuquerque Journal, July 21, 1945, p.2, www.newspapers.com.

18 Henn Archives, *Custodians and Curators*, p.144.

19 Reginald Fisher, "Governor Curry at Lincoln," *El Palacio Volume 54*, April, 1947, p.93.

20 "21,000 for Physicians Approved Here," Albuquerque Journal, June 25, 1947, p.2, www.newspapers.com.

21 "State Historian Plans Reception," Albuquerque Journal, August 29, 1947, p.13, www.newspapers.com.

22 "Ex-Territorial Governor George Curry Dies," Corpus Christi Caller-Times, November 28, 1947, p.12, www.newspapers.com.

23 *Letter from Maurice G. Fulton to Edwin Ferndon*, February 14, 1949, Lincoln County Historical Society Collection.

24 "Mabry to Name Lincoln Memorial Commission," Carlsbad Current-Argus, May 29, 1949, p.7, www.newspapers.com.

25 "In New Mexico," Albuquerque Journal, August 4, 1950, p.6, www.newspapers.com.

26 "Miller Named to Lincoln Commission," Carlsbad Current-Argus, July 6, 1949, p.1, www.newspapers.com.

27 "Billy the Kid Pageant in Lincoln August 14," Albuquerque Journal, June 18, 1949, p.5, www.newspapers.com.

28 "In New Mexico," Albuquerque Journal, August 4, 1950, p.6, www.newspapers.com.

29 "Legislative Summary," Albuquerque Journal, March 11, 1951, p.24, www.newspapers.com.

30 *Executive Order, Office of the Governor, Edwin Mechem*, July 9, 1951, William A. Kehler Papers, University of New Mexico Center for Southwest Research.

31 "Old Lincoln Courthouse Custodian Resigns," Alamogordo Daily, July 27, 1950, p.4, www.newspapers.com.

32 "Mrs. Davis Named Curator-Custodian of Old Courthouse," The Albuquerque Tribune, December 13, 1950, p.22, www.newspapers.com.

33 "Ancestry.com," United States of America, Bureau of the Census; Washington, D.C.; Seventeenth Census of the United States, 1950; Record Group: Records of the Bureau of the Census, 1790-2007; Record Group Number: 29; Residence Date: 1950; Home in 1950: Hondo, Lincoln, New Mexico.

34 "John C. Davis Obituary," Albuquerque Journal, November 1, 2009, p.29, www.newspapers.com.

35 Henn Archives, *Custodians and Curators*, p.148.

36 *Report Covering Activities (The Old Courthouse) Nov & Dec 1951*, Old Lincoln County Memorial Commission, William A. Kehler Papers, University of New Mexico Center for Southwest Research.

37 *Report Covering Activities (The Old Courthouse) Nov & Dec 1951*, Old Lincoln County Memorial Commission, William A. Kehler Papers, University of New Mexico Center for Southwest Research.

38 "Pageant's Billy the Kid Moves to Albuquerque," The Albuquerque Tribune, July 31, 1952, p.22, www.newspapers.com.

39 "Gets New Curator," The Albuquerque Tribune, August 15, 1952, p.1, www.newspapers.com.

40 "Lincoln Museum Plans Open House," Albuquerque Journal, March 19, 1953, p.15, www.newspapers.com.

41 "Old Lincoln County Courthouse Activities in 1952," *El Palacio Volume 60*, February, 1953, p.73.

42 "June Dedication Set for Old Lincoln County Courtroom," The Albuquerque, May 22, 1954, p.10, www.newspapers.com.

43 John Boylan, "Lincoln," Alamogordo Daily, August 19, 1954, p.72, www.newspapers.com.

44 "Memories of Luster Times Return at Courtroom Dedication," Clovis News-Journal, June 21, 1954, p.1, www.newspapers.com.

45 "Old Lincoln Museum Attendance Increases," The Albuquerque Tribune, January 13, 1956, p.24, www.newspapers.com.

46 "Crowds Set New Record at Lincoln," Alamogordo Daily News, August 3, 1955, p.5, www.newspapers.com.

47 "Off the Beaten Path," The Albuquerque Tribune, April 26, 1956, p.11, www.newspapers.com.

48 "New Publication Promotes Lincoln," Carlsbad Current-Argus, September 14, 1955, p.2, www.newspapers.com.

49 "Old Tunstall Store Bought for Museum," The Santa Fe New Mexican, October 6, 1957, p.16, www.newspapers.com.

50 National Register of Historic Places, Nomination Form, *Lincoln Historic District*.

51 *Memo from Nan Boylan to W.A. Keleher, June 8 1962*, William A. Kehler Papers, University of New Mexico Center for Southwest Research.

52 "Introduced in House," The Santa Fe New Mexican, February 14, 1963, p.16, www.newspapers.com.

53 "New Exhibit Dedication at Lincoln," Carlsbad Current-Argus, July 14, 1964, p.10, www.newspapers.com.

54 Henn Archives, *Custodians and Curators*, p.148.

55 *Letter from Nan Boylan to WA Keleher, July 7, 1965*, William A. Kehler Papers, University of New Mexico Center for Southwest Research.

56 *Letter from Nan Boylan to WA Keleher, August 8, 1965*, William A. Kehler Papers, University of New Mexico Center for Southwest Research.

57 *Letter from WA Keleher to U.D. Sawyer, December 16, 1965*, William A. Kehler Papers, University of New Mexico Center for Southwest Research.

58 *Letter from Mrs. Albert R. Booky to WA Kehler, August 20, 1965*, William A. Kehler Papers, University of New Mexico Center for Southwest Research.

59 "Ex Curator of Museum Dies in NM," El Paso Times, September 12, 1972, p.5, www.newspapers.com.

60 *Letter from Paul Gardner to WA Keleher, may 25, 1966*, William A. Kehler Papers, University of New Mexico Center for Southwest Research.

61 "Proposal," Las Vegas Optic, March 11, 1969, p.2, www.newspapers.com.

62 "State Helps Lincoln After Tourism Fails," Silver City Daily, June 23, 1973, p.4, www.newspapers.com.

63 "Lincoln Restoration Study Given Grant," Carlsbad Current-Argus, February 21, 1973, p.3. www.newspapers.com.

64 *Letter from Patricia Ward to Michael L. Keleher, June 13 1973*, William A. Kehler Papers, University of New Mexico Center for Southwest Research.

65 *Letter from Robert O. Anderson to Dessie Sawyer, July 23, 1976,* William A. Kehler Papers, University of New Mexico Center for Southwest Research.

66 "Group Formed to Preserve Southwestern Sites," Carlsbad Current-Argus, April 10, 1977, p.8, www.newspapers.com.

67 "Trim, Centralize State Government," The Santa Fe New Mexican, January 20, 1976, p.1, www.newspapers.com.

68 "Old Lincoln Group Will Stay," Carlsbad Current-Argus, February 13, 1976, p.4, www.newspapers.com.

69 "House Passes Anti-Recession Cash Measure," Carlsbad Current-Argus, February 14, 1978, p.3, www.newspapers.com.

70 *Letter from Michael Keleher to Robert O. Anderson January 31, 1977,* William A. Kehler Papers, University of New Mexico Center for Southwest Research.

71 "Off the Beaten Path," The Albuquerque Tribune, January 27, 1978, p.8, www.newspapers.com.

72 "House Passes Anti-Recession Cash Measure," Carlsbad Current-Argus, February 14, 1978, p.3, www.newspapers.com.

73 "Senate Okays Changes in New Organization," The Roswell Daily, March 13, 1979, p.8, www.newspapers.com

74 *Letter from Phil Helmig to George Ewing May 23, 1979*, William A. Kehler Papers, University of New Mexico Center for Southwest Research.

75 "State Museum Requests $98,000 Budget," The Deming Headlight, October 19, 1979, p.5, www.newspapers.com.

76 "Monuments Need Cash," Carlsbad Current-Argus, June 11, 1980, p.2, www.newspapers.com.

77 "From Upstate Downstate," Albuquerque Journal, Apr 19, 1981, p. 51, www.newspapers.com.

78 "1.4 million Earmarked for Museum Projects," Albuquerque Journal, March 10, 1982, p.20, www.newspapers.com.

79 "Keeping Lincoln Old May Cost $1 Million," Albuquerque Journal, September 6, 1983, p.14, www.newspapers.com.

80 "Renovations Keep Two Historic Lincoln Sites Closed," El Paso Times, July 9, 1985, p.4, www.newspapers.com.

81 Letter to Carl Reed from Thomas Caperton, November 17, 1983. Lincoln Historic Site Archives.

82 Capital Outlay Request Form, CP-RO, Thomas Caperton, Director, NM State Monuments, 1987. Lincoln Historic Site Archives.

83 Lincoln State Monument Maintenance Report, January 21, 1989. Lincoln Historic Site Archives

84 Lincoln State Monument Maintenance Report, October 1991. Lincoln Historic Site Archives; Lincoln State Monument Maintenance Report, May 1, 1994. Lincoln Historic Site Archives;

85 Program Submittal, Lincoln State Monument- HVAC Systems at Courthouse, Tunstall Store, and Visitors Center, M & Engineering, Inc, Santa Fe and Albuquerque, Lincoln Historic Site Archives.

Milton Keynes UK
Ingram Content Group UK Ltd.
UKHW051025110124
435847UK00005B/21